FROM THE AUTHOR

Thank you so much for purchasing this book!
If you have found it helpful, we would greatly appreciate it if you could take a moment to leave an honest review on Amazon. Your feedback will assist others in discovering this book and, hopefully, reaping its benefits as well.

SAMUEL ONUORA

THE BLISS OF IMMORTALITY

Copyright © 2025 Samuel Onuora

ISBN: 978-1-64301-065-6

The opinions expressed by the author in this book are exclusively his and not those of Rehoboth House, Chicago.

NOTICE OF RIGHTS
All Rights Reserved. Reproduction of this material, in whole or part, by whatever means, without the express written consent by the author is not permitted, and is unlawful according to current copyright laws of the United States of America to do so.

BIBLE REFERENCE
Scriptures are taken from various translations of the Bible as indicated, except otherwise.

AUTHOR'S CONTACT:
samuelonuora2017@gmail.com |call +44 7778 652865
Forward all enquiries to Samuel Onuora for counseling, teachings, conferences, seminar and workshops.

COVER AND INTERIOR DESIGNED BY REHOBOTH HOUSE

PUBLISHED IN THE UNITED STATES OF AMERICA
By Rehoboth House, Chicago
rehobothhouseonline.com
info@rehobothhouseonline.com
rehobothpublishing@gmail.com

REHOBOTH HOUSE

TABLE OF CONTENTS

FOREWORD..*v*

INTRODUCTION...*ix*

CHAPTER ONE
The Face And The Image 1

CHAPTER TWO
The New Man..13

CHAPTER THREE
Born Of God/? Yes We Are...31

CHAPTER FOUR
The Redemption of Man..35

CHAPTER FIVE
Resurrection..41

CHAPTER SIX
Evolution of Immortality..71

CHAPTER SEVEN
What Is The New Birth?...79

CHAPTER EIGHT
The Perfect Law Of Liberty...83

CHAPTER NINE
The Anointing...89

CHAPTER TEN
Revelation Knowledge...99

CHAPTER ELEVEN
The Womb Of Immortality...107

CHAPTER TWELVE
A New Consciousness..111

CHAPTER THIRTEEN
Aerodynamic Law And The Law Of The Spirit Of Life.........117

CHAPTER FOURTEEN
Our Immortal Garment..127

CHAPTER FIFTEEN
Questions...135

Foreword

In 1994, while serving my National Youth Service in Sokoto State, the Lord opened my eyes to the subject of life and immortality. I understood this as the eternal purpose of God that the Church has been pre-ordained to fulfil on this earth. Life and immortality are not new arrangements in God; they are finished on the cross. Many things were completed for the Body of Christ, but the Church apprehends these things from one phase to another.

In the eras of the apostolic fathers of the Church, not all that was finished was apprehended, but they saw them dimly for the time to come. It is incredible that even after two thousand years of existence and growth, the Church has not moved beyond the apostles' precepts; yet, precept must be upon precept. By now, all that the apostles saw dimly and darkly that they could not apprehend, the Church ought to have fully apprehended, exhibiting the life of it.

Foreword

Many books have been written in the past that have contributed to the Church's current state. Thank God for this. However, if this generation desires to fulfil the eternal purpose of God, then men must seek THE PRESENT TRUTH, even as it is revealed in this book.

> *"Wherefore I will not be negligent to put you always in remembrance of these things, though ye know them, and be established in the present truth" (2 Pt. 1:12).*

The present truth is the revelation of the Spirit that fulfils the divine purpose of the Spirit in a generation.

The divine purpose for this day is to usher the Church into life and immortality. Truths have been recycled repeatedly in the Church because men do not understand the present truth. The present truth is the dimension of God revealed to the body in a dispensation. We are where we are now to understand the reality of life and immortality.

I love how the man of God, Sam Onuora, defines "understanding" by discussing seeing God in this book. He said, "Seeing God is understanding Him, and understanding is becoming the embodiment of what is revealed."

When understanding the truth is achieved, reality becomes evident physically. Our present challenge is that the Church has been tutored to believe that we will always know in part on this earth. This is a false conclusion. The Church that attains the measure of the stature of the fullness of Christ is a Church that has come into the knowledge and the understanding of the fullness of Christ. Because of the belief that we will always know in part, many destinies have been stranded and unfulfilled.

Let's Briefly Consider This Scripture:

> *"But one in a certain place testified, saying, What is man, that thou art mindful of him? Or the son of man that thou visitest him? Thou madest him a little lower than the angels; thou crownedst him with glory and honour, and didst set him over the works of thy hands: Thou hast put all things in subjection under his feet. For in that he put all in subjection under him, he left nothing that is not put under him. But now we see not yet all things put under him. But we see Jesus, who was made a little lower than the angels for the suffering of death, crowned with glory and honour; that he by the grace of God should taste death for every man. For it became him, for whom are all things, and by whom are all things, in bringing many sons unto glory, to make the captain of their salvation perfect through sufferings." (Heb. 2:6-10).*

You will observe that the scripture above opens up with a question. WHAT IS MAN THAT GOD'S MIND IS FULL OF HIM? This is an age-long question that must be practically answered. The Church cannot escape from this earth without answering this obvious question.

- **MAN IS DIVINE**
- **MAN IS IMMORTAL**
- **MAN IS GOD**

God's mind is full of man because He has reproduced according to His kind.

You will also discover from the above scripture that God set man over the works of His Hands. God gave him dominion over ALL things.

> "Thou hast put all things in subjection under his feet. For in that he put all in subjection under him, he left nothing that is not put under him. But now we see not yet all things put under him."

Note that God put all things in subjection under man's feet and left NOTHING that was not placed under his feet. The apostle declared, in the scripture below.

> "But now we see NOT YET all things put under him."

The works were finished, but men have yet to comprehend what was completed. If all things were put in subjection under the feet of man and God left nothing that was not placed under his feet, then you must understand that death is under man's feet. Man reigns in life without the intrusion of death.

The apostle said, "But now we see NOT YET all things under him." The term "not yet" implies it's ahead. Although we may not see it now, it will surely come.

Jesus tasted death for every man that they might be ushered into glory, even life and immortality.

The man of God, Sam Onuora, an apostle of God, revealed at such a time as this, has been specially wrought by the mighty Hand of God to fulfil His divine mandate in this dispensation. God has equipped him to liberate the Church from the status quo and usher her into this divine glory – Life and Immortality. God has strategically positioned him upon the mountain of the Lord, where everything about this truth is unveiled.

This book, therefore, is a must-read for the end-time Church that the eternal purpose of God might be fulfilled. A transformational encounter and experience with this book are guaranteed.

God bless you

Tayo Oluwaseun Oluwade.

Foreword

Samuel Onuora

Introduction

The revelation of IMMORTALITY is clear and accessible. Once you accept your ground of immortal justification, the revelation of IMMORTALITY opens up to you. You are the RIGHTEOUSNESS of God in Christ Jesus, your JUSTIFICATION. What is the RIGHTEOUSNESS of God? The RIGHTEOUSNESS of God is His Divine essence, which is immortality. Every believer that is born of God is Christ by nature.

Jesus brought life and immortality to light through the gospel after He abolished death and killed sin. The believer is the life and immortality He brought forth. This reality should be clear to us. The believer is the testimony of God embodied in a visible image.

But you see, in the spirit realm of reality, what you do not acknowledge will never work for you. We acknowledge with the heart. To acknowledge is to set truth in view until its reality dawns as consciousness, an experience within your soul faculty. This act of setting in view is a principle in the Spirit called HONOUR.

Honour is the heart posture of giving attention to a matter set before you as you interact with light. This light we interact with is highly intoxicating.

Introduction

Take a look at this scripture below.

> *"Wherefore, holy brethren, partakers of the heavenly calling, consider the Apostle and High Priest of our profession, Christ Jesus" (Hebrews 3:1).*

To consider is to reflect upon or set your gaze upon. It is to look at something steadily with your imagination.

Prayer is not about striving to enter a realm; it is about entering a realm. Prayer is fellowshipping with God, who is light. Staying conscious of God is a form of fellowship, and that is prayer. It completely transports you away from human consciousness into Christ consciousness. It swallows up the carnal mind and opens up the mind of Christ. Prayer is Christ consciousness. Prayer is an interaction with the realities of immortality captured in Christ's mind, which is the intelligence of the Godhead. The Mind of Christ is our garment of light; we must put it on.

> *"Put on your new nature, created to be like God—truly righteous and holy" (Eph 4:24 NLT).*

Prayer for the New Creation Man is never limited to time, place, or space. Prayer is transcendent. The believer is a prayer portal, a ladder reaching all the immortal realities in God and touching the time-bound realm of the earth. This reality becomes our experience as we grow in Christ-consciousness. Do not forget that you are the visible image of the invisible God. That is your immortal identity. We are Portals of Immortality.

Elfrida Onuora.

Chapter One

The Face And The Image

> "Who is the image of the invisible God, the firstborn of every creature: For by him were all things created, that are in heaven, and that are in earth, visible and invisible, whether they be thrones, or dominions, or principalities, or powers: all things were created by him, and for him: And he is before all things, and by him, all things consist. And he is the head of the body, the church: who is the beginning, the firstborn from the dead; that in all things he might have the preeminence" (Colossians 1:15-18).

The Man Christ is the express image of the invisible God. He is the Head of all principalities and powers. He is the One in whom all begotten sons of God are named, the Apostle and High Priest of our profession, the Bishop and Shepherd of our souls, who swallowed up death in victory and brought life and immortality to light. Hallelujah!

Just like the first man, Adam was the gateway of the generations of all fallen humankind. This Man Christ is not just a single person but the gateway through whom the holy generation of the Godman was born. In the day God made Adam, God created all men because their seed was in him. Likewise, in the day God begot the Man Christ Heb 1:4, all the sons of God are begotten. All are in Him, and all are Him.

He is one man of many. He is the Firstborn, whom the race of the Uncreated Ones embodies and proceeds from. This race is the generation of immortals, a people without beginning of days or ending of life, in whom the reality of the Godhead is visibly contained. This Christ race is the immortal reality of Man in God's Divine Predestination. Christ is the Divine Man.

What is Christ?

"Now he which establisheth us with you in Christ, and hath anointed us, is God" (2 Cor 1:21).

Christ is the anointed. Everyone who is in Christ is anointed. God has anointed the saints; therefore, the saints are Christ. So when we say **'Christ,'** we are referring to Him that sanctifieth and they that are sanctified. Both the Head High Priest and the Body Priests, who make the **visible or express image of the invisible God,** are ONE SPIRIT with Him.

In Christ dwelleth the fullness of the Godhead **bodily.** Another word for bodily is **visible. In other words, Christ, the New Man, is the visible expression of God.** He is the express image of the invisible God, the firstborn of every creature. That very image is the throne or glory of God. God's throne is not a seat that God sits on. It is not a "chair" or anything that looks like it. It is the image of His Being. That throne is the centre focus of everything visible (created) and invisible (uncreated). Hence, His kingdom ruleth over all. Everything created stands before that throne that Being; thus, He is before all things.

> *"Who is the image of the invisible God, the firstborn of every creature: For by him were all things created, that are in heaven, and that are in earth, visible and invisible, whether they be thrones, or dominions, or principalities, or powers. All things were created by him, and for him: And he is before all things, and by him all things consist. And he is the head of the body, the church: who is the beginning, the firstborn from the dead; that in all things he might have the preeminence" (Colossians 1:15-18).*

He preexists all things, and He stands before all things. All creation is open and naked before His immortal sight. Everything in creation reports to him, lives and exists by Him. Creation receives from Him and responds to Him. They are fed and sustained by Him. He is the focus of their gaze and delight. By Him, they access the light through which they are sustained. Therefore, they breathe life and show forth His glory in their dimensions.

> *"So that the manifold wisdom of God might now be made known through the church to the rulers and the authorities in the heavenly places" (Eph 3:10).*

It is essential to clarify that Eternity is the home of all created things. Immortality is God. Only God is immortal. So, how does God interface with creatures in Eternity? It is by His throne. His throne is present in every habitable realm of eternity.

> *"The LORD hath prepared his throne in the heavens, and his kingdom ruleth over all" (Psalm 103:19).*

We are saying that this throne is the interface between Eternity and Immortality, between the uncreated God and all creation. His kingdom ruleth over all, meaning His throne is present in all creation. His reign is evident. God reigns by Life.

God, through His throne, communes with His creation. To say you are seated in Christ Jesus, at the right-hand side of the majesty on high, means you are exalted as His revelation and visible manifestation in all creation. This is what it means to be the brightness of God's glory and the express image of His person. The Christ within you is your spirit personality, not the present mortal Adamic physical body you wear. You are not like Christ. You are Christ because your life is Christ. Colossians 3:4. You are immortal as your Father, God.

> *"And hath made us kings and priests unto God and his Father; to him be glory and dominion forever and ever. Amen" (Rev 1:6).*

> *"And hast made us unto our God kings and priests: and we shall reign on the earth" (Rev 5:10).*

This is what it means to be a throne. Our very spirit image is the throne configuration. To be seated is to bear the express image of God. The image is the throne. You are that image. The Immortal Throne is a state of being out of which immortal dominion flows. We reign on the earth unto our God and Father because our kingship and priesthood are of Him, and unto Him, not only on planet earth but in all eternal realms and dimensions.

The Bliss Of Immortality

> *"Blessed be the God and Father of our Lord Jesus Christ, who hath blessed us with all spiritual blessings in heavenly places in Christ" (Eph 1:3).*

You are seated in heavenly places in Christ because you are Christ. There is an Immortal Being who swallows up the old and brings forth the new. He is Jesus Christ; if any man is in Christ, there is a new life. He who is in Christ is Christ because all things in Christ are of God. There is only one spirit.

To be Christ is to be an uncreated life essence. The uncreated life essence is immortality. Immortality is not longevity. It is the uncreated life that is God. A spirit is defined only from the point of view of its life or identity. This life is the law that governs it.

What is our life?

> *"When Christ, who is our life, shall appear, then shall ye also appear with him in glory" (Col. 3:4).*

Our life is Christ; when He appears, we also appear because we are Him, and He is us. ONE SPIRIT. This appearance here is the revelation, manifestation, and demonstration of the divine immortal essence in the body of Christ through the sons of God.

Beholding the Immortal Race

> *"But we all, with open face beholding as in a glass the glory of the lord, are changed into the same image from glory to glory, even as by the spirit of the lord" (2 Corinthians 3:18, KJV).*

In human definition, the face is the front part of the head, but that is not what it means in spiritual terms. The face of a spirit being is its very essence by which it reveals itself. In the immortal reality, the face of God is the revealed image of God. God's face is no longer hidden. It is now revealed. That face or image is what is called the glory of the Lord.

He that is begotten of God is this glory in essence and identity. This means the face you are to behold is your spirit nature because your spirit personality is the express image of God's person, which is the excellent glory of God. There is no way we understand this spirit nature other than to behold the revelation of Jesus Christ.

He is the uncreated, immortal life essence set before us to study in view of who we are. We are saying that the God you are to behold is within you, not without. Therefore, knowing Christ, the Holy Ghost, and the Father is knowing who you are. The Father begat Himself in us, and we reflect the visible essence of His invisible, immortal self to Him. Hallelujah!

> *"But God hath revealed them unto us by his Spirit: for the Spirit searcheth all things, yea, the deep things of God. For what man knoweth the things of a man, save the spirit of man which is in him? Even so, the things of God knoweth no man but the Spirit of God. Now we have received, not the spirit of the world, but the spirit which is of God; that we might know the things that are freely given to us of God"* (1Cor2:10-12).

It takes the Spirit of God to know the things which are of God because these things of God are His secrets hidden within Himself. This secret is now made manifest in Christ. He who is in Christ is made the Quickening Spirit of God. It takes such nature to know, see, and understand the secrets of the Immortal God. This secret is the mystery of God in the New Creation Man, and it is an expression of our honour as kings and priests unto God to discover these secrets and wear them as a crown. This is what it means to know that I may know Him.

Only the Spirit of God, can know the things of God. Knowing in this regard is a consistent inward interaction that culminates in the putting on the consciousness of the new man. We put on the new man by putting on the knowledge of his image. We gaze into the world called Christ, which is our spirit configuration.

> *"But we all, with open face beholding as in a glass the glory of the Lord, are changed into the same image from glory to glory, even as by the spirit of the Lord"* (*2 Corin 3:18, KJV*).

The glory of the Lord is His Face. Remember, Moses asked to see the glory of the Lord. He wanted to see God's face. We have mentioned earlier that the face is not the front part of the head. It is the expressed image of God's person, which is immortality. Moses was seeking the secret of immortality.

'Open Face', as mentioned above, is the spiritual mind. We behold the face image of Yahweh with an open face, the mind (face to face).

We mind the glory of God; we look into the mystery of His essence. Every veil of separation has been taken away in Christ. This is life and peace. The spiritual mind is the mind of Christ.

To be spiritually minded is life and peace. To be spiritually minded is to wear the consciousness of our immortal spirit personality (Christ). To be spiritually minded is to cease from human thinking, reasoning and imagination.

The spiritual mind beholds the Christ within. We set our face (soul) into the face (spirit). We think, speak, imagine, and absorb in stillness the truth and realities revealed in scripture. Our heart interacts as we hear, see, talk and look upon. There is more on this in the latter chapters.

So, with the spiritual mind, we behold those things that are not seen. That is why faith is beholding the "invisible". There is that which is invisible to the carnal mind. Invisible does not mean that which the physical eye cannot see. Initially, the physical senses were designed to interact with all aspects of life. In this regard, nothing created is invisible.

This means that only God is invisible, and only those who share His nature can see Him. Hallelujah! To see him is to understand and embody the knowledge of His reality in the soul region. He who is invisible to all creation is now made visible to the church, in the church and by the Church.

We behold this face (the glory of God) with an open face. The open face here refers to the mind of Christ (immortality), which Scripture says we have. The mind was initially used to engage and document spirit interactions within its sphere of operation. The new man has his mind. His mind is Christ, which is God's knowledge and experience. These realities are willed to the New Man. So when we gaze into the glory, we behold the Man Christ and document His knowledge and experience as God within our soul region. This is what it means to conform. This is not just about knowing God; it is about knowing the things that God alone knows.

Image

This image or identity informs our interactions with the unseen realities of immortality. The soul is to embody the knowledge and experience of the life that you, the spirit, are. As you behold that image, the light of the knowledge of the glory of God revealed in the face of Christ floods the soul and registers therein.

You intentionally switch your mind's focus to the immortal image of yourself, which is the face of God or the life essence of God. As we do, the mind of Christ swallows up the human mind's consciousness. Change our thoughts and patterns from mortal to immortal, carnal to spiritual, human to divine. This is the true meaning of face-to-face. That is what it means to "serve" the Law of God. In Rom 7:24, Paul says with my mind, I serve the law of God.

To serve the Law of God is to attend to it, acknowledge it, to look with a penetrating gaze. Remember that the law of a spirit is the configuration of such a spirit entity, not do's and don'ts. The very frame of such a spirit is responsible for its character and manifestation.

A cherubim is a spiritual law in operation, likewise a seraphim. The New Creation Man is also a law unto himself. He is the law of the Spirit of Life, which is the power of resurrection! So when Paul said, 'That I may know Him and the power of His resurrection,' He was saying that I may understand and embody the laws of the Christman.

This face you behold is the face you are, which you bear. For the new man, beholding God's face is NOT an exercise outside himself. It is a within-interaction. To behold God's face, you must have His face. We behold His face because, by birth, we are His express image. So we are not just beholding a face from afar. We interact with the face we bear. You are not carrying something that you are not permitted to look into. Please ponder this.

The face of the new creation man is that image of God he is through which God illuminates his soul. You are the bearer of His face. His face. His manifold faces and wisdom. By image, you are a custodian of the treasures of immortality.

The Bliss Of Immortality

"But as it is written, Eye hath not seen, nor ear heard, neither have entered into the heart of man, the things which God hath prepared for them that love him. But God hath revealed them unto us by his Spirit: for the Spirit searcheth all things, yea, the deep things of God. For what man knoweth the things of a man, save the spirit of man which is in him? Even so, the things of God knoweth no man but the Spirit of God. Now we have received, not the spirit of the world, but the spirit which is of God; that we might know the things that are freely given to us of God" (1 Cor 2:9-16).

This spirit, which is of God, is the believer. We are the spirit which is of God, and so we can know the depths and secret things of God not just by reading books, but by looking into the pages of His soul.

That is why it is a wasteful adventure to be so consumed in things that do not reveal the reality of that immortal man you are!

God shines in our hearts to give the light of the knowledge of His glory revealed in the face of Jesus Christ, and as you behold this image, you interact with Christ. The knowledge of God's immortal glory is being formed in your soul. This formation is known as **the salvation of the soul**. It is, in reality, a shift or ascension in consciousness. Ascension is a shift in consciousness by the Light. It is not going up!

Remember that as you read this book, the Lord, the Spirit of truth, is with you and in you to enlighten your heart. If your heart is open, He will show you that these things you read are spirit and life. As you examine the material, the Spirit in the words also examines your heart to assess your posture. If your heart posture is right, they will unlock the REVELATION Christ for you. This kind of door does not open unless the heart is childlike. It's your inheritance. Eat it

CHAPTER 2

The New Man

Law Of Identification

We cannot discuss the new man without considering THE LAW OF IDENTIFICATION. The law of identification is the principle of union, a union of natures. That is, two different natures are joined together. One assumes the identity of the other and becomes that other. The law of identification is a principle that holds that when a spirit personality identifies with another spirit, the one that identifies takes on the nature and identity of the one it has identified with.

God brought forth this law, which is as real as every other law in creation.

You take on the identity or essence of him with whom you have identified. The nature of sin defines the natural man's identity because he was identified with sin in Adam. The first man, Adam, identified with Satan and inherited his fallen nature, which is sin. It was Adam who inherited the nature of Satan because he was the one who identified with Satan and not the other way around.

Having identified with Satan, the need arose for Man to be rescued. The only way that could be was for God to identify with Man. God, in the person of the last Adam, identified with Man in his fallen state and inherited the fallen nature of man.

> *"For ye know the grace of our Lord Jesus Christ, that, though he was rich, (IMMORTALITY) yet for your sakes he became poor,(MORTALITY) that ye through his poverty might be rich (IMMORTAL")* (2 Corinthians 8:9 KJV).

God is identifying with Man in his lowly estate. According to this scripture, God became poor so the poor man could be rich. It is essential to understand what God is rich in. God is RICH IN GLORY, WHICH IS LIFE AND IMMORTALITY.

> *"And now, O Father, glorify thou me with thine own self with the glory which I had with thee before the world was"* (John 17:5, KJV).

This reality is the wealth of God - glory. This glory is His immortality. He alone holds this mystery. He has never and will never share this with anything created or any being created.

In the scripture above, Jesus asked for the glory of immortality. But the wonderful thing is that He asks for that glory as a man. Why would a man be asking for immortality? This glory was the same thing Moses had asked for, but he was denied it.

Who is this man, and what was He asking for?

He was asking for something beyond returning to what He had been as the Immortal Word of God. In this scripture, he asked for the thing predestinated in the divine scroll concerning man: that humanity should be admitted into the fellowship of the Godhead. He was asking for Man to carry the glory of God bodily.

The image of the new man is defined in the light of this very glory. The immortal glory of God

> *"Father, I will that they also, whom thou hast given me, be with me where I am; that they may behold my glory, which thou hast given me: for thou lovedst me before the foundation of the world" (John 17:24, KJV).*

The Lord of Glory identified with Man to become what man could not become for himself. The original intention of God was for Adam to become this immortal glory. However, because Adam could not meet the demands of this inheritance, God sent Jesus to obtain it for humanity. What Jesus became at resurrection was for man. He received the most excellent name for Man. He brought man into the Communion of Immortals.

In this place where we are, there is only ONE SPIRIT, ONE LIFE, ONE THRONE. The Father, the Word, the Holy Ghost and the Saint all occupy ONE THRONE. That is why it is ONE who sat on the throne. That ONE is a harmony of beings with ONE NATURE and bears ONE NAME, having ONE BODY dwelling in ONE TABERNACLE with ONE HIGH PRIEST.

There is no other spirit but one. God is Man. Man is God—one substance. There can never be a separation. It happened by the Law of Identification.

The Christ Man

> *"For we know the grace of our Lord Jesus Christ that though he was rich..."*

What is God rich in? To understand who the new man is, we must view this scripture. The man was to be identified with the immortal God in the person of Jesus Christ, who became us. It is what the scripture means: *'If any man is in Christ, he is a new creation.'*

Do not forget that when Adam identified with Satan, Adam became what Satan is. When God identified with man, God became what man is.

Why do you now think that if Man identifies with the Immortal God, he will remain the mortal man he is?

"If any man is in Christ, it means he identifies with God, and the old self ceases to be. A new spirit, possessing the full immortal attribute of uncreatedness, is brought forth to replace the old man who passed away. Such a being has appeared at the beginning with the uncreated God." This New Creation is before all things. He is before all beings. He is before all creation. He has neither the beginning of days nor the ending of life. His priesthood is after the power of an endless life. Whether they be thrones, dominions, powers and principalities, the new man is before them all and above them all. His ancientness is God. God is His age. He is at the beginning of God. That is why John the Apostle says,

The Bliss Of Immortality

> *"That which was from the beginning, which we have seen, which we have heard, which we have looked upon, and our hands have handled, of the word of life" (1 John 1:1).*

The beginning he is talking about here is immortality. It is where nothing created can approach, yet John says he is in fellowship with this immortal reality.

Brethren, your fellowship with God is the basis of your identity. You have not begun to tap into the riches of His fellowship until you accept and acknowledge your immortal identity.

God joined Himself to man in their fallen state. This is the poverty of God. To become poor is to be made Man. No matter what a man owns as material possessions, if he is not alive in the immortal reality, he is poor because a spirit possesses nothing outside himself. To say that a spirit is alive means it is aware of or enlightened by God and responsive to His immortal light realms.

So when the mortal man identified with God, the poor death-doomed Adamic Man ceased to be, and a new man emerged from the transaction. The outcome of this experience is a man who is God by spirit configuration. Yet one thing remains for this man: to come to the understanding of his God-nature. The conscious awareness of his immortal identity must register in his soul, or he would live like a mere man.

Brethren, whoever is joined to the Lord is one Spirit with him. It is the law of identification. By this, we are Christ because we are One Spirit with Him.

Sonship And Joint Heirship

The contention the Jews had with Jesus was His claim of sonship. They were angry with Jesus because he called himself the Son of God! Do you know why? It is because they understand THE IMPLICATION OF SONSHIP. Sonship is oneness. The begetter and the begotten are ONE.

In the Jewish context, the son of a person has access to and ownership of everything that such a person owns. They knew that for a man to claim the fatherhood of God, he was saying He and the Father share the same glory, throne, nature, authority, name, and inheritance. What blasphemy! The Jews believe that God does not share His glory with any man. Why would the son of a carpenter claim their God to be His Father? It was an insult to them!

God does not share His glory with the fallen man, but He has given that glory to the new man. Everything God gave to Jesus Christ is given to Man. That is joint heirship. Because of the new birth, we are partakers of the divine nature. This nature is the glory of God. It is essential to know what the glory of God is.

The Glory Of God

We have said that God is rich, and His glory is his riches.

> "Who being the brightness of his glory, and the express image of his person, and upholding all things by the word of his power, when he had by himself purged our sins, sat down on the right hand of the Majesty on high" (Hebrews 1:3, KJV).

The glory of God is His being! When you hear "glory", it refers to the very being and image of God! The scripture above states that Jesus is the brightness of God's glory and the exact representation of His person. This very brightness of God's glory and the expressed image of God's person is what the believer is in Christ.

A spirit is not separate from its riches. The riches of a spirit being are its being. It is fallen human beings that glory in perishables. Spirits are measured by the substance of their makeup, which is within them. A spirit has nothing outside of its being! That is why God can take away this earth and bring forth a new one. That creative ability is within His being. That is riches.

If any man identifies with Christ, he has identified with the brightness of God's glory and the express image of God's person. It is the image from which Dominion issues forth. In the beginning, when God told Adam to have Dominion, God spoke to the image within him to bring forth reign and government upon the earth. The image is a Throne and Dominion.

Jesus, the Son of God, became the brightness of God's glory and the express image of His person, who upholds all things by the word of His power. That upholding is the function of the image he has become. This image is the visible body form of the invisible Godhead. In Christ dwelleth the fullness of the Godhead bodily. This is the inheritance that Christ obtained for humanity. This visible image is the inheritance of anyone who is born of God. It is an immortal body of light made of the Divine DNA.

Spirits are light entities. Every Spirit is a kind of light. God is light, and He is the Father of lights. That means He is the maker of lights. He made lights and spread them all over eternity, but the light He gave birth to is immortal in the class of Himself, the Uncreated One. The New Creation is the immortal light of Yahweh. He is the effulgence of God to all things created. In Him, God became visible! It is what it means to believe in the Son of God. You identify with Him and take on His nature. What a privilege it is to be a man! It is why the angels admire and honour you!

A New Self Ephesians 4:24

Just as the rod of Moses swallowed up all the Egyptian snakes, and they were no longer there, the man Christ receives a mortal man, and the man loses himself in the identity of Christ. The old Spirit ceases to be, and a new Spirit, Christ, is born.

That is why the Bible says old things have passed away. The old self passed away when he identified with Christ. A new self was born. This new self is the brightness of God's glory and the expressed image of His person - the Christ-You.

This new man is the visible Body of the Divine God. The believer in the immortal reality is the visible body image of the invisible God. Philemon verse 6 says every good thing in Christ is in you.

> "I am crucified with Christ: nevertheless I live; yet not I, but Christ liveth in me: and the life which I now live in the flesh I live by the faith of the Son of God, who loved me and gave himself for me" (2:20, KJV).

Do you notice there are two "I's" here?

The first "I" represents the old man.

> "Since the children have flesh and blood, he too shared in their humanity so that by his death he might break the power of him who holds the power of death—that is, the devil" (Heb 2:14, NIV).

The second "I" represents the Christ-man.

The believer is the second "I."

The Son of God gave His "Self" for the old "Self."

The first self is the image of death.

The second self is the image of immortality.

The second self is the express image of God, which is the Christ within you. The first "I" is the mortal nature of the fallen man, and the second "I" is the immortal nature of God. The first 'I' is corruptible, but the second 'I' is the incorruptible seedword of God.

Jesus knew no sin; God made Him sin, which means He never had fellowship with sin but was innocent of evil. He was the spotless Lamb of God who took away the sin of the world.

Sin nature was imputed to Him, this precious Lamb. Sin's nature is corruption and mortality. So God made Him sin that we might be made righteous in God through Christ Jesus. The righteousness of God is His glory and immortality. This glory and immortality are the essence of the believer's identity. We are the Godman.

> *"For in him dwelleth all the fulness of the Godhead bodily. [10] And ye are complete in him, which is the head of all principality and power" (Colossians 2:9-10, KJV).*

This immortal man, whom we are, the fullness of the Godhead, dwells in him bodily, meaning visibly present. This visibility means God is now made manifest (1 Tim 3:16).

Do you know that the Body Jesus wears now is the very Body we are? That Body is within your spirit essence, waiting to swallow up the Adamic Body. It is the mystical Body of everyone who is born of God. We are members of Him, flesh and bone. This is life and immortality. Eph 5:20.

Just as the human race proceeded from the first man, Adam, so too do we, the Church, proceed from Christ. In the same way, Adam called Eve the flesh of his flesh and the bone of his bone; we are the flesh of Christ and the bone of His bone. We are His sacred Body. Brethren, do you know the meaning of the phrase 'Body of Christ'?

Body means the visible component form. Therefore, the New Creation is the express or visible image of the invisible God. It is why the scripture says:

> *"To the intent that now unto the principalities and powers in heavenly places might be known by the church the manifold wisdom of God" (Eph 3:10).*

The Church is the entity through whom the manifold wisdom of God will be made known to principalities and powers. In reality, this is the Body of Christ.

Body means garment or suits sprouting forth from essence. The garment is not separated from the being! The garment is what gives expression to the being. It's a living garment. With this garment, Jesus ascended the Holiest of all to offer His blood to the Father for all humanity, once and for all. Without that Body, He could not perform that priestly worship. A priest must be clothed and not naked; his Body is his garment and tabernacle.

In this visible being, called Christ, is the Body (Church) and the Head (The Lord). It refers to the Sanctifier and us whom He sanctified. These two are one in God.

> "By the which will we are sanctified through the offering of the Body of Jesus Christ once for all" Hebrews 10:10, KJV).

Sanctification is a resurrection experience. He that is sanctified is he that is resurrected. Resurrection is not a future event. Resurrection is Christ. If any man is in Christ, he is in that Day called resurrection. Jesus Christ is our Daystar and our Resurrection Morning. We are in His Day, that Day in which the Father begot Him.

As He Is

> Herein is our love made perfect, that we may have boldness in the Day of judgment: because as he is, so are we in this world" (1 John 4:17, KJV).

The new man is not a spirit personality that is different from who God is. All the abilities of God are inherent in Him because He is God in human form. God is the Body, the visible form of the invisible God—the fullness of the Godhead dwells in Him. God created mighty and powerful beings, but gave birth to His very Self in the New Creation.

At the resurrection, we could see the tokens and wonders of the resurrected man we have become. Let's ponder these scriptures:

As He is, so are we in this world. Luke 24:30-31.

"And it came to pass, as he sat at meat with them, he took bread, and blessed it, and brake, and gave to them".

And their eyes were opened, and they knew him, and he vanished from their sight.

As He is, so are we in this world. John 20:26

"And after eight days again, his disciples were within, and Thomas was with them: then came Jesus, the doors being shut, stood in the midst, and said, Peace be unto you".

As He is, so are we in this world. Acts 1:9.

"And when he had spoken these things, while they beheld, he was taken up, and a cloud received him out of sight"t.

As He is, so are we in this world. John 21:5-6.

"Then Jesus saith unto them, Children, have ye any meat? They answered him, No. And he said unto them, Cast the net on the right side of the ship, and ye shall find. They cast, therefore, and now they were not able to draw it for the multitude of fishes."

The Bliss Of Immortality

As He is, so are we in this world. Rev 1:12-16.

> *"And I turned to see the voice that spake with me. And being turned, I saw seven golden candlesticks; And in the midst of the seven candlesticks one like unto the Son of man, clothed with a garment down to the foot, and girt about the paps with a golden girdle. His Head and his hair were white like wool, as white as snow; and his eyes were as a flame of fire; And his feet like unto fine brass, as if they burned in a furnace; and his voice as the sound of many waters. And he had in his right hand seven stars: and out of his mouth went a sharp two-edged sword: and his countenance was as the sun shineth in his strength".*

For as He is, so are we now.

Why would the Lord appear to the churches in this manner? What was He communicating to them by His looks? Jesus is the identity of the Church. The Head is the reality of the Body, so when He shows up in this manner, by that appearance, He is communicating to them WHO THEY ARE and WHAT THEY ARE.

The thickest veil upon the minds of many is the inward posture of separating the believer from the Lord Jesus: Jesus is powerful and the Almighty, but the believer is weak and helpless. It is because many have failed to accept that Christ is our new self.

People say, 'Do not expect me to do that. I am not Jesus Christ.' This statement stems from an attempt to belittle the finished work of God and distance the new creation man from God, who is now His reality. It is a denial of the immortal capacity invested in the Godman. It is a detachment of the Immortal Head from the Immortal Body. It is simply saying that whatever is in the Head remains in the Head. The Body does not enjoy such access and authority as the Head. It is a denial that God has come in the flesh. Meanwhile, the Head has willed all power and authority to the Body, and His government rests upon His shoulder.

Why did Jesus say we would do greater works than He did? Why is Christ made unto us wisdom and righteousness, sanctification and redemption? What are the effects and implications of this truth? What are the impacts and implications of identification with Him in His Immortal Divinity? Why did He say to us, 'I go unto my Father and your Father; to my God and your God?' What is the meaning of that joint ownership, joint-heirship, as reflected in these words of Jesus Christ the New Man?

One of the reasons the Church is not yet demonstrating Dominion is the core of a belief system that is deeply ingrained in the minds of many. There is a belief system that subtly says we will be like Him one Day after we have fulfilled specific demands. We will be like Him when we get to heaven. We will be like Him when we have obeyed all His instructions. We shall be immortal one Day when Jesus comes.

But truth says we are as He is NOW, and when we see Him as He is, we shall be like Him. This statement seems contradictory, but it is not. We are as He is, yet our awareness is still rooted in human consciousness. So, as we continue to behold Him as He is in us, our consciousness shifts, and our soul takes on the proper shape. Soul means documented knowledge or experience, and the New Creation man is not just a nominal Christ; to Him, all the experiences of the immortal God are willed in immortal reality.

Our life, our walk, our thinking and imagination, our decisions, and our utterances all flow from that reality as we acknowledge it and focus on Him, who is our life.

His coming or rapture that many are waiting for is not first a coming in the sky, but a glorious appearance in the Body, in as many as feast on the realities of His power, which is at work in the saints. We are not the ones waiting for the coming of Jesus. The reverse is the case. Jesus is waiting to reap a harvest of sons who will come into the full regalia and functionality of their Melchizedek Priesthood here on earth. Sons who would activate the resurrection force, whose voice would cause many dead to rise again unto life Eternal. Hallelujah!

So, His love overwhelms us as we gaze steadily on this truth. It is from this love that our obedience flows. We do His will because we are in fellowship with the understanding that we have no other will except His. He worketh in us both to will and to do of His good pleasure. We are one Spirit with Him and have no separate feelings, emotions, thoughts or imaginations. God is our Life.

The light that we are in Him conditions our soul into the order of immortality and shuts down every high thing that exalts itself against the knowledge of God so that pure living waters can flow out of us freely. Those waters are the realities of our Godlife that gush forth ceaselessly as we focus on our identity in God.

Acknowledging the truth of the finished work is the very beginning foundation and the perfecting truth of an effectual walk in Dominion. The same truth awakens us to our reality as God on earth and purifies us from vain mortal thinking patterns that hinder our fruitfulness in righteousness.

Identity

> "And we know that the Son of God is come and hath given us an understanding, that we may know him that is true, and we are in him that is true, even in his Son Jesus Christ. This is the true God and eternal life" (1 John 5:20, KJV).

The issue of identity is so crucial in this season because the Dominion of God must flow into all creation and to the uttermost parts of the earth. Dominion will not flow until the understanding of our IMMORTAL IDENTITY is established in our hearts. We cannot wield the sceptre of righteousness until we understand that our very being is the throne from which God's dominion rests.

This new man is a member of the council of divinity. He had inherited all the experiences of God before anything was created. So you inherited his eyes, and all things in creation are open and naked before your eyes. Though this may not be your experience in your present consciousness, but without doubt it is your reality and experience in Christ.

May The Lord Give Us Understanding

There is nothing in creation that is beyond you as the New Man. The secrets of all creation are coded within your being because your existence predates creation. Cherubim operations, for instance, are locked up within them and will not find expression until the sons of God take their place. There is no secret in creation that we cannot access if we set our hearts to know. Your Father has given all things to you.

Created spirits are given to serve us, and we engage them in receiving their ministry. How? By the words we speak, principally. We speak words that activate their operations around us. We acknowledge the Lord's provision of them.

We recognise that we are in Zion, the city of God, amidst an innumerable company of angels, and we thank Him for this supply. Yes, we can speak with them and provide instructions when needed.

Their ministry to us is based on our immortal reality in God, and we receive as much as our present level of understanding allows us to grasp. Yes, the present limitation of our mortal Body necessitates their ministry to us, but as we grow in knowledge, it becomes clear that they need us for proper functioning.

The truth is that these beings, as majestic as they are, stand in awe of you because they know who you are. They know your capacity. They are delightfully at your service forever. This is not a boast but a celebration of the fatherhood of immortality.

So, the greatest deliverance that will happen to you is A SHIFT OF CONSCIOUSNESS from human to divine.

- From mortal to immortal
- From corruptible to incorruptible
- From man to God

This shift occurs as we set our hearts on looking into the Perfect Law of Liberty, our very being. What we are called to examine is within our being. We look within. We look above within. Our above is within.

We learn to look inward and be drawn into the consciousness of Christ within us. There is a life to be explored. There is a reality to be touched.

He has given us eyes to read immortal scrolls and show forth the glories of His wisdom to all creation. We can explore the secrets of light that were previously unapproachable. We dare to explore You, Our Immortal Father!

Never forget. We are not learning to become. We are learning to know and become consciously aware of who we are so that we can function as the Christ on earth.

We are the New Man!

CHAPTER 3

Born Of God? Yes We Are

"Therefore, the Jews sought the more to kill him because he not only had broken the sabbath but said also that God was his Father, making himself equal with God" (John 5:18).

Two key points emerge from the scripture above regarding Jesus and His Jewish brothers. I want to point them out here:

- Jesus called God His Father
- The Jews sought to kill Him

Why Did Jews Seek To Kill Jesus?

They said He called God His Father. The Jews understand the concept of Sonship from the perspective of their culture. Do not forget that God committed His oracles unto them, so they understood the implication when Jesus called God His Father. That was the reason for their rage.

Listen To What They Said:

"Not only had He broken the sabbath, but said also that God was His Father, making Himself equal with God".

When Jesus called God His Father, He claimed to be in the same class as or equal to God. The issue of sonship is related to identity or DNA. When you say that a man is your Father or that someone is your son, you are simply saying that you are naturally equal to the person.

From that angle, the Jews judged the affirmation of Jesus in the scripture above. The complete program of a man's life is contained within the DNA of the one who gave birth to him. Everything included in God's DNA is PRESENT in the DNA of His son, thereby making His Son equal with him. This is real inheritance. DNA is inheritance.

The reason why the Jews were angry with Jesus when He called God His Father is that they understood the meaning of what Jesus said. What Jesus meant was that He is one with God. In other words, He meant that He shares nature, identity, glory, throne, and life essence with their Yahweh, whose name they cannot pronounce because of reverence. To them, man could not be born of God, but to God, it is possible. Was Jesus lying? No. On what ground do believers call God their Father? Hear what Jesus said concerning the believers.

Joint Heirship

"I ascend unto my Father, and your Father; and to my God and your God". John 20:17

Did You Hear That?

'I ascend to my Father and your Father.'

If God is His Father, it means that He embodies the fullness of God by nature, and that same God whom He calls His Father is your Father, too. It also means that you are an embodiment of God's fullness from birth. We are Immortal Sons of God by birth. The New Creation Man had never existed before.

> *"Of his own will begat he us by the word of truth... which liveth and abideth forever" (James 1:18, 1 Peter 1:23).*

The Scripture says that the testimony of God concerning His Firstborn Son is in us who believe in the Son. Many of us call ourselves believers, yet when what we believe in is unveiled, we disagree. This has to change.

> *"And this is the record, that god hath given to us eternal life, and this life is in his son. [12] he that hath the son hath life; and he that hath not the son of god hath not life" (1 John 5:11-12).*

What is referred to as eternal life here is, in reality, the Immortal DNA of God.

Please Look At The Scripture Below.

> "*Of his own will begat he us with the word of truth, that we should be a kind of firstfruits of his creatures*". *(James 1:18).*

We did not journey from being a living soul to becoming a life-giving spirit. We were born life-giving spirits. God is by nature the father of the race of the life-giving spirit. If our Father is God, we are God. If our father is Immortal, we are Immortal.

This does not suggest independence from Him or a denial of His Fatherhood over us. Instead, it is oneness with Him. We are in union with the God of glory.

There is nothing in creation that crosses breeds. There is nothing that God created that can change its natural life essence into another life essence in its true nature. Everything created gives birth to or produces offspring after its kind. God is not different. We are not just his kind. We are His life.

> "*But he that is joined unto the Lord is one Spirit*" *(1 Corinthians 6:17).*

> "*For both he that sanctifieth and they who are sanctified are all of one: for which cause he is not ashamed to call them brethren...*" *(Hebrews 2:11).*

Truth is not found in the traditions of men but in the reality of God, the truth.

What is reality? Reality is that divine, incorruptible life essence which cannot change. God is that life, Christ Jesus is that life, the Holy Ghost is that life, the Believer is that life.

CHAPTER 4

The Redemption of Man

"He that heareth my word, and believeth on him that sent me hath everlasting life, and shall not come into condemnation, but is passed from death unto life" (John 5:24).

This is the story of Man's Redemption. God, who existed in Himself, created eternity and brought forth celestial beings and places. He beautified that space with an artistic array of light entities in various celestial places of His dominion.

God needed one who would reflect Him without inhibitions in all His works. He needed a visible image. He needed a body for self-expression. He needed a house of His glory where His manifold wisdom would be demonstrated to all creation visibly.

This image had existed in His soul before the world's foundation as a living reality waiting to be brought forth.

So when God created Man, God brought to visibility what existed in His heart before the worlds were made. This was not an afterthought. Man existed in the heart of God before the foundations of the world. Man was God's dream and prophecy waiting to be revealed. God created Man in His image to become His expressed image.

This first man was not the express image of God. He was to be after feeding on the Tree of Life. The expressed image of God is immortal and cannot die. Was Adam perfect? In the state he was in, yes, but because of what he was meant to transition into, no. He was perfect because everything God created was created good and perfect. Every good and perfect gift comes from God, the Father of lights. Let's remember that Lucifer was perfect on the day he was made, yet he fell when iniquity was found in him.

> "Thou wast perfect in thy ways from the day that thou wast created, till iniquity was found in thee" (Ezekiel 28:15, KJV).

Adam was created a LIVING SOUL BEING to transition from that state into another state of being through the operation of God's life. If that had happened, all humankind would have become the seed of God, because the entire human race was unborn within Adam. So, in him, the entire human race existed in seed form. They were IN HIM.

All his experiences and interactions with trees in the garden directly affected His generations IN HIM. If Adam had fed on the Tree of Life, he would have transited from the state of a living soul being into a state of being called a LIFE-GIVING SPIRIT.

The human race in him was to be born as IMMORTAL BEINGS and not as FALLEN SOUL BEINGS. That state would have been an automatic birth state for his children in his loins.

But instead of Adam submitting to the Tree of Life to feed on it, which would have immortalised him, he turned and had communion with a fallen wisdom called Satan. That tree of Knowledge was a tree of light, the light of death.

That tree was a tree of wisdom, so it was attractive and alluring. Scripture holds that Eve found the tree attractive. She found that it could make her wise.

> *"And when the woman saw that the tree was good for food and that it was pleasant to the eyes, and a tree to be desired to make one wise, she took of the fruit thereof, and did eat, and also gave unto her husband with her, and he did eat" (Gen 3:6).*

Wisdom is brightness, ravishing beauty. It is the crown of reign and the sceptre of rulership. Do not forget that Satan was said to be full of wisdom and perfect in beauty. This beauty is an effulgence of wisdom which was supposed to minister life, but became corrupted. Sin is a corrupted life found in the entity called Satan. So, that tree offered a kind of wisdom: the wisdom of sin and death.

Having submitted to the corrupt influences of this tree, Eve ate and gave to Adam. In doing that which God forbade them to do, they died and became mortals in sin and death. The human race, in Adam, was also mortalized with him because they were in him.

The Redemption of Man

"For as in Adam all die, even so in Christ shall all be made alive" (1 Corinthians 15:22).

The scripture above states that all died in Adam. To die is to become mortal, subject to sin, death, sickness, disease, and corruption. Mortality is the soil in which everything that is of Satan finds expression in man and through man.

The scripture above also states that in Christ, all who die in Adam shall be made alive. To be made alive is to become life; LIFE is Immortal. It means that even though Adam fell, he was not irredeemable. Why? Adam was created to transit, so he was a work in progress. Satan was a completed work of creation, and every step he took was a well-calculated move against God's authority.

So, Adam was working on something that needed to be completed, which was why redemption was possible. The man was a work in progress, and even though that work did not stop, it became corrupted and expired; therefore, it needed to pass away.

The coming of God in the flesh in the person of Jesus Christ, who became the last Adam or the finishing Adam, was for the fulfilment and perfection of that which God dreamt of, which He began and set in motion in the beginning when He made Adam. Jesus moved from the last Adam and became Christ, the God-Man. Old things have passed away, and BEHOLD, all things are now New and of God. The New is of God.

All who experienced MORTALITY in Adam are called into IMMORTALITY, which the last Adam became when He was justified in the Spirit because of his obedience to the will of God.

The Bliss Of Immortality

Justification is man's IMMORTALITY.

There is an 'in Him' in Adam by which all human race fell into corruption and mortality, but another 'in Him' in Christ by which all human race is translated into immortality and incorruptibility. In both cases, one man took responsibility for an action that touched the destiny of an entire race. If any man who died in Adam believes in Christ, he shall not perish but has passed from mortal to immortal. Glory!

Adam's experience of MORTALITY was an experience for all who died in Adam; in the same way, Jesus' experience of IMMORTALITY is an experience for all who are made alive in Christ. Hallelujah!

> *"Therefore, as by the offence of one judgment came upon all men unto condemnation; even so by the righteousness of one, the free gift came upon all men unto justification of life"* (*Rom 5:18).*

Every man born of a woman made of the seed of Adam came into this world a premature man or woman. We all came into the world as mortals, but are to be made LIFE AND IMMORTALITY in Christ Jesus.

Take A Look At This Scripture Below

> *"And if Christ be in you, even though the body is dead because of sin; but the Spirit is LIFE because of righteousness"* (Romans 8:10).

The Spirit you is LIFE. That is what the Righteousness of God, which was imputed to you at New Birth, made you. That is what is stated in the scripture above. You are not just alive. You are LIFE. To be Life is to be IMMORTAL. We are IMMORTAL BEINGS. We are not celestial beings. Celestial beings are created sons of God. Immortal beings are BEGOTTEN SONS OF GOD.

CHAPTER 5

Resurrection

"Jesus saith unto her, Thy brother shall rise again. Martha saith unto him, I know that he shall rise again in the resurrection at the last day. Jesus said unto her, I am the resurrection, and the life: he that believeth in me, though he were dead, yet shall he live: And whosoever liveth and believeth in me shall never die. Believest thou this? Then Martha, as soon as she heard that Jesus was coming, went and met him, but Mary sat still in the house. Then said Martha unto Jesus, Lord, if thou hadst been here, my brother had not died. But I know that even now, whatsoever thou wilt ask of God, God will give it thee. Jesus saith unto her, Thy brother shall rise again. Martha saith unto him, I know that he shall rise again in the resurrection at the last day. Jesus said unto her, I am the resurrection, and the life: he that believeth in me, though he were dead, yet shall he live: And whosoever liveth and believeth in me shall never die. Believest thou this? She saith unto him, Yea, Lord: I believe that thou art the Christ, the Son of God, which should come into the world" (John 11:23-26).

Jesus tells Martha that the resurrection is NOT an event in the future. However, Jesus is the resurrection and the life, and whoever believes in Him comes into the experience of the resurrection and the life. The reality of resurrection is encapsulated in the man Christ. He is the resurrection and the Life; as He is, so are we in this world.

So, what should be the posture of our hearts? We look into this Resurrection Man so that we might KNOW HIM and the power of His Resurrection. To know Him is to know You.

What is this power? The power of His resurrection is the Spirit that raised Christ from the dead, quickening our mortal bodies. The Lord is that Spirit; we are joined to Him as ONE. The power of resurrection is the Christ-Life that you are. This is our victory over death.

What Is Resurrection?

Resurrection is not a journey out of the grave. If a journey out of the grave is what resurrection is, it means that Lazarus is the fruit of the dead. This means that he experienced resurrection before the justification of Jesus in the spirit.

In this scripture, Jesus boldly declares Himself to be the Resurrection and the Life. In other words, He is the resurrection of all men that died in Adam. Resurrection is beyond a return from death. It is the swallowing up of death by life and the revealing or birthing of newness such that the dead is of a different quality of life from that which was resurrected or birthed forth. So Jesus was raised from the dead as a new man with a new life and authority. Resurrection is the birth of God in a man's structural formation.

The Bliss Of Immortality

Many believers believe that resurrection is when they will put off this mortal physical body and put on the immortal body. It is clear and true that many believers look forward to experiencing resurrection in the future. To some, resurrection is a rapture experience. Please wake up to the reality of the finished work.

How would you react if I told you you had already experienced resurrection? If Jesus is the resurrection and the life, and you have been made as He is, it means you are the resurrection. When a person believes in Christ, they do not just receive Christ. He becomes Christ, and all that Christ is becomes His reality.

What will your attitude be to people around you if you genuinely know that you have already experienced resurrection? Resurrection is life, immortal life.

Resurrection is not something to experience in the days ahead, as Martha said to Jesus. Jesus Himself is the last day because every dead person is brought to life in Him. He is the end of Man, the Last Man.

"For unto which of the angels said he at any time, Thou art my Son, this day have I begotten thee? And again, I will be to him a Father, and he shall be to me a Son?"(Heb 1:5).

Man is an evil day, and Jesus is the end of that day and the beginning of another day called 'THIS DAY'. He is the ascended one—the brightness of immortal glory. The Bible says in Rev 22:3 that there is no need for light in the city because the Lamb is the light of the City. The Lamb is the Day of the Lord.

The Father says of Him, 'This day have I begotten you.' God Almighty gave birth to an Immortal Man. All who believe in Him are raised to live in that One Man. He is the Beginning and the Ending. In Him, God and man found a meeting point.

- Resurrection is a state of being.
- Resurrection is the righteousness of God now.
- Resurrection is not an experience in the future.
- Resurrection is God's appearance in the flesh as Man, not as the last Adam but as the resurrected Man.

The word future does not exist in the volume of the book "The Perfect Law of Liberty." There is no such thing as a future in the immortal reality. We are in Him, who is the beginning of all creation now. So, what is the future then?

The word "future" is a fallen word used as a reference for events yet to occur in the present time zone. That an event has not occurred in the time zone does not mean it did not happen. The new man does not live in this zone. So, His realities are ever-present, not time-bound. His experience and manifestation of the resurrection are not tied to time. It is tied to the discovery of himself in the resurrection. The word 'future' is not part of our language. We don't say the future. We say now. We are in the day of the Lord now; His day is immortality.

'Future' for us is to manifest the God that we are for creation to behold and be delivered, and this is not subject to time but our ability to hasten the day of the Lord into appearance. We are to put on the knowledge of the resurrection and cause life to spring forth in creation. Resurrection is the revelation of God in the structure of man.

The New Man is the future of the whole creation. He is what creation is waiting for. He is the event that must happen in creation. We are the future, if there is anything as a future, because we are one with Him, who is the beginning of all things created, of whom Himself has no beginning.

The New Birth Resurrection

Resurrection is referred to as a new birth experience or new birth reality. Your new birth experience is your resurrection reality. You are the resurrection. You are life.

The new man is resurrection and life. He is not bound to time frames. He is without beginning or end. The reality of Christ, the one who was, who is, who is to come, is the reality of him who is the I am. The same yesterday, today and forevermore, the unchanging one. Soon, you will realise that yesterday, today, and tomorrow are all part of the present. They all coexist.

That is why experiences can be re-engaged and re-experienced, and they could be re-entered into something so real and so fresh. You moved into the eternal dimensions to touch that ever-present reality. Eternity is within you, and you can experience these realities as you engage with the principles of their operations. This is known as a remembrance.

What is Remembrance?

Jesus said to His disciples; *"...Eat my flesh, drink my blood and do this in remembrance of me."*

What was He saying?

This is beyond the act of eating bread and drinking wine as a memorial or religious activity. It is more of an inward experience that outward activity is meant to bring us into. In this regard, remembering is not just about getting back a forgotten experience or recalling something to memory. It is not just to remember Jesus once in a while.

It is to live within the consciousness of Christ as our ever-present experience and reality. Remembrance is the ever-presentness of a reality. Jesus says to continue experiencing the reality of resurrection until your consciousness is fully immersed in its newness. Its newness is its newness.

Keep the record of your resurrection reality in your heart and revisit it often. Let your sight be captivated by this reality. As you contemplate me, you are learning to overcome the power of corruption. You are learning to mount up on wings. You are learning to fly, for there are places within you beyond time, and as you remember me, your consciousness is transported into these places of pleasures, secrets that are held in the immortal reality of the Resurrection Man.

To remember the Lord is to experience him in the immortal reality. This is what it means to eat his flesh and drink his blood.

- His presentness
- His nowness
- His unchangingness
- His I amness becomes a living consciousness that defines your operations

The New Creation Man will come into the experience of remembering the beginnings of creation and those that predate it. This means that the exclusive experience of God as the creator you have inherited as a Son becomes registered in your soul as a documented reality.

You live as a now and forever being who is not waiting for the future to come but is bringing the realities of immortality into creation for the redemption of time. All beginnings and all endings are collapsed into that entity called the New Creation Man.

He is the total of all lights, ages, beginnings, and civilisations. All the experiences of God are his to explore.

What I am saying is that Time is a limiting factor. An illusion that does not exist in the eternal dimensions and the immortal realms where the New Man dwells. He who is above is he who is timeless and ageless. He who is timeless and ageless cannot be measured with the instrument of time. He is forever young. He does not age because He is not bound by time.

Life Without Measure

> *"The thief cometh not, but for to steal, and to kill, and to destroy: I am come that they might have life and that they might have it more abundantly" (John 10:10).*

Man became limited at the fall of Adam. A counted and measured being whose existence on the earth as an embodied entity came under the calibrations of time. But Jesus came to change this order so that people might live bodily on the earth forever. That time should no longer shrink the bodies of men, but that mortality should be swallowed up by the more abundant life of God that has been given in Christ.

> *"For he whom God hath sent speaketh the words of God: for God giveth not the Spirit by measure unto him" (John 3:34).*

The measure of a thing is the limit of its capacity. The New Man in Christ is without limits. God is His measure. God is in His stature. God is His fullness.

The New Man is a man without measure. He is not a limited man. The forces that cast boundaries upon the mortal man have no hold on him. You are the boundless and bountiful man. The curse of the fallen man is his limitation and incapacity, but the blessing of Christ is His boundlessness and almightiness.

The Timeless Man

What some call the future is already a present reality for an immortal. The difference lies in that one is time-bound, time-restricted, and time-conscious, whereas the other is timeless and immortal. One is waiting for time, and the other is riding above time. Choose your reality. Time consciousness and time constraints are consequences of the fall from which Jesus delivered us. We need to desire and learn to walk in the reality of this deliverance if we are to fulfil the mandate of delivering creation from the bondage of corruption. When the consciousness of our reality is built in us, we lose time consciousness and cease to be confined, defined, measured and constrained by time.

We would be more aware of our ever-presentness, which is immeasurable by time. This means that your five minutes in time can be five months in the glory.

Your '35 years' in bliss can be 35 minutes in time. When this reality becomes our consciousness, how can we age? In this reality, the sun does not smite because one brighter than the noonday sun shines here - the son of righteousness.

The smiting of the sun is an operation of ageing and corruption, but the bright morning starlight is the operation of freshness and youthfulness.

> Psalm 110:3 says, "In the beauties of holiness from the womb of the morning thou hast the dew of thy youth. Hallelujah!!

The new man is not a product of years, days and months. He is not measured according to the Earth's movement around the Sun. He is on the day of the Lord; He is the I am.

Back to our discussion, resurrection is a living person, and that person is Christ. Anyone who is joined to this Christ becomes the resurrection as Christ is.

- You are the resurrection.

- Understand that you are Christ.

- Yield your heart to the resurrection life

- Feed on the knowledge of this resurrection life

- Build the consciousness of this resurrection life until even the body is swallowed up by the resurrection force.

Jesus, the Passover Lamb, said to Martha, *"I am the resurrection and the life."*

Martha's mentality concerning the resurrection is the same as that of many believers today - an event yet to come.

The words holiness and righteousness define our resurrected being in the immortal reality.

Hear What Martha Said In The Scripture John 11:23-26

(Vs 23) "Jesus saith unto her, thy brother shall rise again.

(Vs 24) Martha saith unto him, I know that he shall rise again in the resurrection at the last day..."

Jesus was not referring to a journey out of physical death, which Lazarus experienced that day, but to something much more profound. What could it be?

You can see that Martha did not understand the concept of resurrection. To her, resurrection is an experience that mortal men call the future or the last day. Christ is the future to all who died in Adam. Christ is the future of all living creatures. Our language is life, not the future. Christ is that life that I am. I am Christ, the resurrected new man.

(Vs 25) Jesus said unto her, I am the resurrection, and the life: he that believeth in me, though he were dead, yet shall he live:

Jesus told Martha that He is the Resurrection and the Life. Where are you now if he is indeed the resurrection and the life, and you are in him? You are in the resurrection and the life.

If he is the resurrection and the life indeed, and you are as he is, what are you now? You are the resurrection and the life.

(Vs 26) And whosoever liveth and believeth in me shall never die. Believest thou this?

This idea of not dying is a significant issue today. The Jews rebuked Jesus for teaching the possibility of not dying. The 21st-century church displays the same attitude the Jewish people manifested before Jesus. They kept on shouting:

'This is a hard saying, Jesus. Who will believe this reality, Jesus?'

Resurrection is what God promised Abraham. No record anywhere in the creation points to gold, silver, and cattle as what God promised Abraham.

God spoke to Abraham and said, In your 'seed', shall all the nations of the earth be blessed.

Blessed With What? Check the Scripture in Genesis Below.

> *"And in thy seed shall all the nations of the earth be blessed; because thou hast obeyed my voice" (Genesis 22:18).*

The seed of Abraham is the ark that conveyed the resurrection and the life, which is the immortal nature out of its immortal state into time for all nations to be blessed with it.

The Concept Of Rapture

> *"And inasmuch as it is appointed for men to die once and after this comes judgment, so Christ also, having been offered once to bear the sins of many, will appear a second time for salvation without reference to sin, to those who eagerly await Him" (Heb 9:27-28).*

The second appearance of Jesus is not the first appearance in the sky but in the sons. When the scripture declares that the whole creation is waiting for the manifestation of the sons of God, it is saying that creation is waiting for the revealing of God in the sons' bodily form, because until the bodies of men are transformed, creation cannot witness deliverance. So rapture is the clothing of men with a resurrected body, which is the swallowing of mortality by immortality.

In other words, the rapture is the appearance of God in the flesh. The Rapture occurs when Jesus is resurrected and given an immortal body. Graves of dead men opened because resurrection power opened the gates of hell to deliver prisoners of death. Once again, that operation of resurrection power shall be unleashed, and that is what the Rapture is.

Saints on earth will grow into the full stature of their sonship. They will be clothed with their immortal bodies, and by that operation, they will harvest souls unto God and bring about heightened manifestations of life in the body of Christ. This is the sounding of the trumpet, the message and the manifestation of LIFE in the saints' BODILY. This is what will trigger the second coming of the Lord. Then graves would be opened again, and the bodies of saints who slept shall be changed.

Those who slept in Christ shall arise and take up their bodies to be changed into immortal bodies. When God begins to show forth in men BODILY, the rapture occurs when the saints are fleshing out the mystery of deathlessness.

See Second Corinthians 15: 51-57

> *Behold, I tell you a mystery; we will not all sleep, but we will all be changed, in a moment, in the twinkling of an eye, at the last trumpet; for the trumpet will sound, and the dead will be raised imperishable, and we will be changed. For this perishable must put on the imperishable, and this mortal must put on immortality. But when this perishable will have put on the imperishable, and this mortal will have put on immortality, then will come about the saying that is written, "DEATH IS SWALLOWED UP in victory. "O DEATH, WHERE IS YOUR VICTORY? O DEATH, WHERE IS YOUR STING?" The sting of death is sin, and the power of sin is the law, but thanks be to God, who gives us the victory through our Lord Jesus Christ.*

'In a moment, in the twinkling of an eye,' this is a metaphor for the season in which this operation of God is being carried out in the sons.

'At the Last Trump' refers to a kind of message that would fill the body of Christ: those eagerly waiting to see this reality manifest. The trumpet of God is a message. It is a dimension of truth embedded with the power and operation of transfiguration. It is a season coming upon the church for transfiguring men to put on the immortal priestly garment.

Behold The Manifold Wisdom.

- There are three "days."
- The day of Adam.
- The day of Satan.
- The Lord's Day.

We must understand what each day represents to comprehend God's plan concerning humanity. Suppose we are ever going to conquer religion and project the reality of the finished work of God in Christ Jesus. We also need to understand that the religion practised among believers has its roots in the day of Satan, which is his reign over God's creation.

Please Follow Me Carefully To The End.

The earth and all its inhabitants were created and given to Adam by God. We have this record in the book of Genesis. Let us see some aspects of this record in the scripture below.

The Bliss Of Immortality

> *"And God said, Let us make man in our image, after our likeness: and let them have dominion over the fish of the sea, and over the fowl of the air, and over the cattle, and over all the earth, and over every creeping thing that creepeth upon the earth" (Genesis 1:26).*

> *"And God blessed them, and God said unto them, Be fruitful, and multiply, and replenish the earth, and subdue it: and have dominion over the fish of the sea, and over the fowl of the air, and over every living thing that moveth upon the earth" (Genesis 1:28).*

The scripture does not mention how long Adam's reign lasted over creation. But one thing is sure: he ruled and reigned over all God put under him. Psalm 8 says that Adam was crowned with glory and honour. Creation enjoyed the expressions of the love of God on the day of Adam. There was peace and harmony among the creatures. Creatures loved one another until that very moment when iniquity entered Adam. It was a moment of agony for all creatures; their Lord fell out of alignment with God the Creator.

That moment of agony brought an end to the day of Adam upon creation and ushered in the reign of sin (Satan). Check the scripture below for confirmation of the beginning of the day of Satan that was ushered in from the point of the fall of Adam.

> *"And the devil, taking him up into a high mountain, shewed unto him all the kingdoms of the world in a moment of time. And the devil said unto him, All this power will I give thee, and the glory of them: for that is delivered unto me; and to whomsoever I will I give it." (Luke 4:5-6).*

In this scripture, Satan told Jesus that the earth's sphere of glory and the authority that governs it were delivered to him. The question is, who delivered it to him?

Check The Scripture Below:

> *"What is man, that thou art mindful of him? And the son of man, that thou visitest him? For thou hast made him a little lower than the angels, and hast crowned him with glory and honour. Thou madest him to have dominion over the works of thy hands; thou hast put all things under his feet: All sheep and oxen, yea, and the beasts of the field; The fowl of the air, and the fish of the sea, and whatsoever passeth through the paths of the seas" (Psalm 8:4-8).*

The scripture here says that God crowned man (Adam) with glory and honour, so Adam was the man to whom God delivered the glory and the power of the earth sphere. It is this same glory and power over the earth sphere, as said in Luke 4, that was delivered to him. God gave it to Adam, and Adam gave it to Satan. The day of Satan began to reign from the point of the fall of Adam. A new civilisation was ushered in upon the earth and its inhabitants. Love and peace were withdrawn from the earth. The season of hate and bitterness was brought over creation.

This new civilisation, which emerged from creation, hacked into the DNA of creatures and corrupted them. It entered Adam and killed him together with his generation yet unborn who were within his loins.

Adam's death was for all because all humans were in him when he died. There was no such thing as individual death. It was one who all died. So also, in another, all shall be made alive. This is manifold wisdom in operation. All the fall spirits could not decode the operation of this wisdom. It was beyond their compensation, so they crucified the Lord of glory.

Check The Scripture Below

> "For as in Adam all die, even so in Christ shall all be made alive" (1 Corinthians 15:22).

- For in one (Adam), all died.
- In one (Christ), all shall be made alive.

God consecrated Adam as god over the earth sphere, and Adam turned his God-given authority and glory over to Satan. From the moment Satan became the God of the earth. It was on this ground of dethroned and enthronement between Adam and Satan that qualified Satan to attend the meeting on the created sons of God in Job 1 and 2. Check the scripture below.

> "Again there was a day when the sons of God came to present themselves before the Lord, and Satan came also among them to present himself before the Lord" (Job 2:1).

Adam used to attend that meeting as the God of the earth, but the moment he turned his power over to Satan and became the next god of the earth sphere, Adam stopped attending, and Satan began to attend the meeting in his place. There is more to know, brethren.

Follow Me Carefully To The End, Please

In the day or reign of Adam, nothing died, nothing aged, and there were no sickness or disease. Creation experienced newness under the reign of Adam. If the dad of Adam had continued, we would not be talking about sickness and disease today. There will be no physical death, corruption, or ageing; no one will count age because age is a form of depreciation and decay.

This Truth Should Be Clear To Us

The reign of Satan is the reason for physical death, ageing, spots, decay, wrinkles, sickness and disease, and corruption. The entrance of sin into the world as a natural phenomenon brought about all the above experiences. To stop all those experiences, God would have to come to the earth as a man and remove sin as a nature, which is the root cause of all the calamities mentioned above. This will help us understand the scripture below.

> *"For then must he often have suffered since the foundation of the world: but now once in the end of the world hath he appeared to put away sin by the sacrifice of himself"* (Hebrews 9:26).

This scripture clearly states that Jesus CHRIST came at the entrance of "age."

What "age"? Whose "age"?

The age mentioned there is the reign of Satan. That age was expiring. That was the reason why men who lived in it counted their days. That will help you understand what King David meant when he said the Lord should teach them to distinguish between good and evil. Their day was the day of Satan. All men that came out of Adam lived under the day of Satan, both Jews and Gentiles.

Check This Scripture Below For Confirmation

> *"For we have before proved both Jews and Gentiles, that they are all under sin"* (Romans 3:9).

Did You See That Scripture?

Everything that lived in the day of Satan experienced ageing, physical death, sickness and disease, spots, wrinkles, and blemishes. Jesus came to terminate the reign of the day of Satan and ushered in His day or government, which has no end. Hebrews 9:26 says He came to remove sin by sacrificing Himself at the end of the age/day.

Behold The Lord's Day

If the Lord succeeds in removing the sin nature, that will mean the end of Satan's day over man. But if he failed, the reign of Satan would continue. That will help us understand the reason why Satan was busy following and tempting Him to stop Him. The scripture says that Satan tempted him at all points but found no fault with him. Jesus is my hero.

He removed the sinful nature from the world. That is one sure thing his sacrifice accomplished for all who died in Adam. The destruction of sin is his sure victory, which guarantees salvation for all men. He did not just remove sin; he put it to death, meaning that the thing called sin does not exist anymore.

There are motions of sins, and there is what is called the sin nature. The sacrifice of Jesus removed sin, according to Hebrews 9:26. It will take renewing the mind, with the knowledge of immortality revealed in Christ, to purge the works of the flesh or motions of sin from the physical body. That is the reason for 2 Corinthians 4:6: For God, who commanded the light to shine out of darkness, hath shined in our hearts, to give the light of the knowledge of his glory revealed in the face of Jesus Christ.

When this knowledge is enthroned in the soul faculty, the body will naturally stop gravitating towards bad habits. It is a sure way; try it and see the victory of the cross in manifestation.

The Day Of The Lord.

The ushering in of the day of the Lord is sure proof that the day of Satan over creation has expired. The day of the Lord began from the point of His justification. The death of all men was not an individual death; all died in one man, Adam. Similarly, the justification of all men was not a personal experience. All of humanity was justified in one man, Christ. The day Adam died was the day all died. So also, the day Christ, the immortal NEW MAN, was born was the day we were all born.

Take A Look At This Scripture

> *"For unto which of the angels said he at any time, Thou art my Son, THIS DAY HAVE I BEGOTTEN THEE" (Heb. 1:5).*

The Bliss Of Immortality

GOD gave birth to all in one, the same way Satan killed all in one. Jesus was born as the immortal new man on the same day all believers were born. The reality of this birth experience is why the scripture says that the sanctifier and those sanctified are all of one: why? All were born one day in one Man, Christ. The reason for this is that the priests must come out of the loins of the High Priest. Christ is the High Priest, and we are the priests.

We celebrate the day of the birth of the Lord, our High Priest, for in him we were born. The day of our born-again experience was not the day we were born. We were born together with our High Priest. It is a day that has no beginning or end. That is an operation of righteousness, Melchizedek. This birth on the day of the Lord is a total departure from the day of Satan and the experiences within that day. The prayers of men and women who lived and died under the day of Satan are not allowed in the day of the Lord.

Our age is the Lord's age. Our life is the Lord's life. Our garment is the Lord's garment. Our throne is the Lord's throne. His birthday is our birthday, for we were born in Him on the same day. Our birthday is not an experience in time. It was an experience in him that is life and immortality.

Created creatures did not witness our immortal birth because it did not occur within their sphere. That is why celestial beings could not recognise Christ when He ascended to the Father from the earth.

> *"Lift up your heads, O ye gates; and be ye lifted up ye everlasting doors; and the King of glory shall come in. Who is this King of glory? The Lord strong and mighty, the Lord mighty in battle. Lift up your heads, O ye gates; even lift them up, ye everlasting doors; and the King of glory shall come in. Who is this King of glory? The Lord of hosts, he is the King of glory. Selah" (Psalm 24:7-10).*

Physical birth is an experience that is related to mortal men. It is not our experience. Our birth is an immortal experience in the womb of immortality.

The Rapture Generation

> *"And not only they but ourselves also, which have the first fruits of the Spirit, even we ourselves groan within ourselves, waiting for the adoption, to wit, the redemption of our body"* (Romans 8:23).

This scripture highlights some essential realities that should not be overlooked. What are these realities?

- It states that we have the firstfruits of the Spirit
- It states that we are waiting for the adoption, which is the redemption of the body.

What is the first fruit of the Spirit? Another word for first fruits is first begotten from the dead. The person referred to as the first fruits or the firstborn is the resurrected Godman. There is a man who is God now in creation. The scripture above says that we have the first fruits of the Spirit. That scripture says, "We are the first fruit of the Spirit". In other words, the fullness of the Godhead contained in Christ is also embodied in our spirit personality. You remember the scripture says that in Christ dwelleth all the fullness of the Godhead bodily, and we are complete in Him.

Check The Scripture Below

> *"That the communication of thy faith may become effectual by the acknowledging of every good thing which is in you in Christ Jesus" (Philemon 1:6).*

This book of Philemon says that the good things embodied in Christ are also in us. You have to be one spirit with the first begotten to be able to house his Immortal treasures. So, Paul, in the above scripture, said that we have the first fruits of the Spirit, which is what he referred to as spiritual blessings in heavenly places in Christ Jesus. Did you notice how all the scriptures are connecting? It will take an immortal spirit to embody the immortal riches of the immortal God.

Paul said that we groan while in this present physical Adamic body. Why? You may never understand what this groaning is until the knowledge of your immortal spirit personality dawns on you. As an immortal spirit, you need a body to find expression in creation. You need an immortal body to officiate as an immortal priest within creation. Your operations are highly limited through this earthen vessel, the physical body. The spirit you has its kind of body, so the groaning calls for our immortal body to come out of our spirit to swallow this present body up.

That is a RAPTURE EXPERIENCE. It is the appearance and manifestation of God upon the earth, spirit, soul, and body. Just as Christ appeared on earth after the resurrection with a glorified body inhabited by the immortal spirit bearing God's experiences (soul), in the same way, many saints would physically come into this order. That was the experience Paul the Apostle sought. He called it the resurrection of the dead. He expressed his desire for it in the scripture below.

> *"If by any means I might attain unto the resurrection of the dead" (Philippians 3:11).*

Apostle Paul saw this experience of body transition from the present state to the immortal, glorified body of the new creation man, and he went after it. He saw that the way to it is through the knowledge of Christ. The natural life and its beauty lost value to Paul because of his reality of the body's redemption from corruption. He further said that he was reaching for the high calling in Christ.

Check The Scripture Below

> *"Yea doubtless, and I count all things but loss for the excellency of the knowledge of Christ Jesus my Lord: for whom I have suffered the loss of all things, and do count them but dung, that I may win Christ, I press toward the mark for the prize of the high calling of God in Christ Jesus" (Philippians 3:8,14).*

This experience is available for all. Those who have seen it live for it. Those who have not seen it live to fulfil their ministry and 'go to heaven', and some, for material things, corruptible things of this world.

Back to our main discussion, the fact that believers still experience physical death, ageing, sickness, and disease does not mean that it is normal. Do not forget that the scripture says death is the last enemy to be destroyed. Death here captures spots, wrinkles, sickness, and disease: physical death, ageing, and blemishes. The generation of believers that will subdue these expressions of death is the rapture generation. I am pleased to announce to you that the Rapture Generation is here.

Let's Consider This Scripture Again

> *"Because the creature itself also shall be delivered from the bondage of corruption into the glorious liberty of the children of God. For we know that the whole creation groaneth and travaileth in pain together until now. And not only they but ourselves also, which have the firstfruits of the Spirit, even we ourselves groan within ourselves, waiting for the adoption, to wit, the redemption of our body" (Romans 8:21-23).*

Corruption is a force of death that affects all creatures on earth, resulting in the physical deterioration of creatures, ageing, sickness, disease, spots, wrinkles, and blemishes. If you carefully look at creation, you will see corruption in operation.

Who Will Deliver Creation From This Mortal Experience?

The scripture says that it is the responsibility of the sons of God. The sons of God cannot embark on this rescue operation to creation with this mortal garment, physical body. We must put on our Melchizedek righteous immortal garment, our heavenly body. Check the scripture in the next page.

> *"For in this, we groan, earnestly desiring to be clothed upon with our house which is from heaven: If so be that being clothed we shall not be found naked. For we that are in this tabernacle do groan, being burdened: not for that we would be unclothed, but clothed upon, that mortality might be swallowed up of life" 2 Corinthians 5:2-4*

We groan in this mortal Adamic body but shall not groan in our immortal Melchizedek garment. In our immortal garment, creation will see us as we are in our immortal state of being, glory. Apostle Paul said, "For the sake of this experience, I count all things but loss for the excellency of the knowledge of Christ" What do you seek? What do you live for? What do you see as the reason for your being on earth now? If you are not living for this purpose, you are lost in Babylon.

We Shall Not All Sleep

Please read the scripture in 1 Corinthians 15:51-55: *"Behold, I shew you a mystery; We shall not all sleep, but we shall all be changed."*

What mystery is Apostle Paul calling our attention to in the above scripture? He said, " Behold, I show you a mystery". The mystery is a rapture experience; this Adamic body gives way for the immortal body of the new man to take its place.

In verse 52 he said; *"In a moment, in the twinkling of an eye, at the last trump: for the trumpet shall sound, and the dead shall be raised incorruptible, and we shall be changed."*

He said this experience would happen through the operation of the last Trump, and the word Trump here conveys a message. What is this message? This message fully reveals the TREASURE IN THIS EARTHEN VESSEL, PHYSICAL BODY. This treasure is the incorruptible, uncreated, immortal identity of God. This treasure is the visible image of God. This treasure is the resurrected life. This treasure is expected to swallow up this corruptible mortal body.

> *"For this corruptible must put on incorruption, and this mortal must put on immortality" 1 Corinthians 15:53).*

The mystery is that the incorruption, which is to be put on, is already inside the corruption. So, incorruption shall come out of the corruption and swallow it up. What a glorious experience!

> *"So when this corruptible shall have put on incorruption, and this mortal shall have put on immortality, then shall be brought to pass the saying that is written, Death is swallowed up in victory" (1 Corinthians 15:54).*

You can now see that this experience ends all operations of death, the last enemy to be destroyed. It is the joy that creation has long awaited. Creation knows that an experience like this is on the way, so it is groaning and calling for the manifestation of the sons of God.

> *"O death, where is thy sting? O grave, where is thy victory?" (1 Corinthians 15:55).*

> *"For the Lord himself will come down from heaven, with a loud command, with the voice of the archangel and with the trumpet call of God, and the dead in Christ will rise first. After that, we who are still alive and are left will be caught up together with them in the clouds to meet the Lord in the air. And so we will be with the Lord forever" (I Thes 4:16-17, NIV).*

Let's take a close look at the scripture above: it clearly states that the Lord will come from heaven with a loud command, accompanied by the voice of the archangel and the trumpet call of God. It means He will come with a sound. That sound is already sounding for those who have an ear.

Did you notice that the Lord will come and not an angel? The Lord will not send any of His created angels because the message of life and immortality is not committed to created angels to proclaim. Why? It is not their life or identity. I have heard many say that when the Lord shall come again, Jerusalem will be His landing place. No. We do not find such a record in Scripture. His landing place is His present dwelling place, our spirit personality.

His voice shall be heard in all nations where believers are. Any city where believers are not, that city is doomed because His voice will not be heard there. The word "rapture" captures wholeness, which implies an immortal spirit, an immortal body, and an immortal consciousness in the soul. What kind of body do you think the saints that resurrected with Christ came out of their graves with? It could not have been the same Adamic body that was buried. They were resurrected with the same immortal body that Jesus had been resurrected with. Their work was cut short in righteousness to attain that resurrection experience with Jesus.

The scripture above also states that the Lord will come with the Trump of God. What is the Trump of God? It means the message of God. It is the totality of the gospel of evolution of immortality or the complete revelation of the personality of God in his immortal reality. This revelation has been released in dispensations, but a time will come when its fullness will be allowed to flood and cover the earth. This message will bring about a change of clothing, a new body. The scripture says that we shall be clothed and not be found naked. The change of body which took place in the grave shall be experienced outside the grave before what is known as the general experience of rapture.

Those who will come into this glorious experience are the generation of believers who will deliver creation from the bondage of corruption mentioned earlier. The message of life and immortality encompasses all aspects of divinity. It is a message that reveals the GODHEAD's visible and invisible reality. We are now in that season, brethren. The trumpet of God is now sounding within His treasure in the earthen vessel. The rapture generation is given the message of our immortal identity to proclaim in the hearing of all creation. NOW IS THE TIME.

We Are The Rapture Generation

The MESSAGE GIVEN TO US TO PROCLAIM makes us the rapture generation. The message captures the fullness of the revelation of the manifold immortal treasure within the earthen vessel, life and immortality. The best was reserved for the last. We are in for a glorious moment in the history of creation. It is

Resurrection

the season for the collective MANIFESTATION of that which every believer embodies within their Immortal spirit, personality, LIFE, AND IMMORTALITY.

See you in this glorious experience

CHAPTER 6

Evolution Of Immortality

Immortality is not first about the longevity of the human physical body. God does not want an immortalised Adamic body. He has judged and destroyed the Adamic race. What God is doing is replacing the expired, death-doomed body with a new glorified body, the body of the New Creation man, sprouting forth from our heaven, the Christ-You. God, by His Spirit, is giving life and peace to the mortal Adamic body, not to immortalise it but to swallow it with Life eventually. The same thing God did with the spirit man, He is doing with the soul and the body: Life shall swallow them completely.

So immortality would result in longevity, but that is not what it is like in the first place. It has nothing to do with the longevity of the human Spirit because the human Spirit will never cease to exist, whether in death or life. That also goes for all spirits, both living and dead.

Angels of God who kept their estate have all lived beyond millions of what the fallen man calls years, yet that has not immortalised them. Immortality is a divine exclusive.

The last Adam resurrected an Immortal New Man, yet he did not even live up to 50 in time before he switched to immortality.

The experience of the man Enoch was not an experience of immortality. Yes, Enoch was translated. This experience animated his body and kept it alive in the eternal realms of life, but his translation did not recreate his dead Spirit.

In his translation, he was still a mortal man who needed to be made alive in Christ, and he was made alive after Jesus conquered death. If Enoch experienced immortality, Jesus would not have been the first fruit of all creation. The Bible says God took Enoch, but does it say He took Enoch into Himself? Only Jesus was taken into the Father. That is what it means to be immortal in the light.

> "No man hath seen God at any time; the only begotten Son, which is in the bosom of the Father, he hath declared him" (John 1:18).

> "But now is Christ risen from the dead, and become the firstfruits of them that slept. But every man in his own order: Christ the firstfruits; afterwards they that are Christ's at his coming" (1 Cor 15:20,23).

Enoch's translation does not make him a new creature, even though his body experienced no corruption. Through fellowship with God, he became absorbed by the realm of light he was fellowshipping. God took him, but he was not taken into God. Can a man be in the present heaven bodily? From the experience of Enoch and Elijah, the answer is yes.

However, this is not to be compared with the NEW BIRTH EXPERIENCE. Enoch walked with God, and his body did not see death; instead, being the seed of the first Adam, he needed regeneration. He had a testimony of faith. He walked with God, but scripture holds:

> *"And these all, having obtained a good report through faith, received not the promise: God having provided some better thing for us, that they without us should not be made perfect"* (Heb 11:39-40).

What Enoch obtained was a good report, not the promise. He, too, rejoiced to see the day of the Messiah! He waited for the promise of perfection in Christ Jesus—life and immortality.

The height of bliss and pleasures is not just to be taken by GOD like Enoch, but to be taken into GOD as Christ was. There are places in the eternal realms of God that a man can be raptured into by communion. However, it is impossible to be taken into the immortality of Him, who alone dwells in the light, without the very nature of that immortality.

Jesus boldly declared, 'I go to the Father'. He secured this for all humanity at the right hand of the Majesty on High.

Enoch still needed to experience a transition from mortality (Adam) into immortality (Christ) through the resurrected Christ. Enoch has seen Christ, so he is immortal now with a glorified immortal body, not even the same body with which he left the earth, but the very living-bread body of the Quickening Christ. Hallelujah!

- Immortality is a state of being.
- Humanity is a state of being.
- Mortality is a state of being.

Immortal Realities

> *"You have been regenerated (born again) not from a mortal origin (seed, sperm) but from one that is immortal, by the ever-living and lasting word of God" (1 Peter 1:23).*

The word 'humanity' is used to capture the race of a living, mortal soul. Immortality, God, Eternal life, I Am, and Divinity are words used to capture an uncreated LIFE ESSENCE (the creator of all).

That is why He is the only one in the entire universe who ALONE HAS IMMORTALITY, dwelling in the light that no creature can approach. Mortality is a state of being dead spiritually or of being out of alignment with God.

While Adam was in Eden, he was neither mortal nor immortal. When Jesus was born to Mary on this earth, he was neither mortal nor immortal. He became mortal when God made Him sin and became immortal when He was justified in the Spirit.

> *"For he hath made him be sin for us, who knew no sin; that we might be made the righteousness of God in him" (2 Corinthians 5:21).*

According to this scripture, Jesus was made sin, which means He became mortal. It became possible for Him to die. The scripture also states that the reason why He was made sin was for men who were mortals to be made the righteousness of God.

To be made in the righteousness of God is immortality. Righteousness is the state of being in the very FORM of God. Jesus did not go through a process to become human. He was born so. He also did not go through a process to become sin or mortal. It was imputed at the fullness of His time on earth.

Hebrews tells us that as the children were partakers of flesh and blood (in their human state), He also partook of the same.

> *"Forasmuch then as the children are partakers of flesh and blood, he also himself likewise took part of the same" (Heb. 2:14).*

> *"Who, being in the form of God, thought it not robbery to be equal with God: But made himself of no reputation, and took upon him the form of a servant, and was made in the likeness of men" (Philippians 2:6-7).*

If any man is in Christ, he is a new creature. This scripture in 2 Corinthians 5:17 is the conclusion of the whole matter. To be a new creature is to be Immortal. On the part of mortal man, becoming immortal through Jesus is not a journey or a process. It is an automatic experience.

But there is a process (of eating and chewing) required for laying hold on the knowledge of the nature of life and immortality, which brings about the expression of that immortal life, even to the point of the redemption of the body. Our seasons and dealings are this one thing: to know what we have been made in Christ Jesus and show it forth as a manifest reality.

See The Following Scripture:

> For this is good and acceptable in the sight of God our Saviour; Who will have all men to be saved, and to come unto the knowledge of the truth" (1 Timothy 2:3-4).

The First Verse Mentions "To Be Saved."

Saved from what? Saved from mortality state. After this immortal experience of being born of God, the New Man is instructed to come to the knowledge of the truth. What is the truth? The truth is Christ. This Christ is the Spirit of the New Man. This Spirit is immortal, born of the Immortal God. The created man, who became mortal because of his disobedience, gave birth to mortals in his fallen image. The immortal, uncreated God gave birth to the Uncreated Immortal Son in His express image, who is far above the heavens, far above all death and corruption, and in whom all the many Sons are named with immortal identity.

> "Of his own will begat he us with the word of truth, that we should be a kind of firstfruits of his creatures James" (1:18).

> "But he that is joined unto the Lord is one spirit" (1 Corinthians 6:17).

The New Man is Christ. He is not to be known by the appearance of the temporary Adamic body he wears. We can know this man only as He is in spirit essence, not after the flesh. Through this perspective, the body can receive proper care and be brought into the service of righteousness until its ultimate redemption.

The Bliss Of Immortality

The believer is the Uncreated Immortal Son of the Uncreated IMMORTAL God. It is not mere CONFESSION but a confession based on the KNOWING that brings a BELIEVER into AWARENESS of his IMMORTAL UNION with DIVINITY. This should be an experiential knowledge.

Until we begin to acknowledge this truth about our identity and set our gaze upon it, believers will continue to experience the effects of Adam's fall. Until our consciousness is consumed into this one thing, OUR ONENESS WITH LIFE AND IMMORTALITY, a whole lot of things would remain muddled up: kings would continue to die like mere men and princes of Zion would continue to trek while slaves ride on horses. God forbid.

Evolution Of Immortality

Reflection Point

Personal Notes:

Guided Action Plan

CHAPTER 7

What Is The New Birth?

The NEW BIRTH is fulfilling the vision that God conceived within Himself before the creation of ETERNITY and its INHABITANTS (creatures).

This vision of God was conceived and concealed within the WOMB of IMMORTALITY, kept from the eyes of all living creatures within ETERNITY.

> "But as it is written, Eye hath not seen, nor ear heard, neither have entered into the heart of man, the things which God hath prepared for them that love him"(1 Cor 2:9).

According to the scripture, He prepared not for those who love Him but those whom He loved with His everlasting love, who have received His love. The Christ-man (we) is God's beloved and begotten son. He is the Son of Love.

In this reality that we are born into, our first assignment is not to love God. We are to receive the knowledge of His love and enjoy

His love. That love is the light of our very being. God is love, and so are we. When we see this, we can truly reflect His love back to Him and all creation.

Of the fullness of His love have we all received, grace for grace. The New Man is not called to come and love God. We were called to enjoy God's love. It is His love we enjoy that flows from us back to Him.

> "Behold, what manner of love the Father hath bestowed upon us, that we should be called the sons of God" (1 John 3:1).

It is a religious thing to put up a fleshly expression and call it love for God. God is not the author of religion. Satan is. We are not called to please God. We are born to experience His Immortal pleasures. Give up your WORKS and lay hold on FAITH. Lay hold of the light of life that you have received and watch yourself burn with immortal pleasures and ecstasies forevermore. Until you have enjoyed the love, you cannot express it in its purest form as it is embedded in your God nature. You are love, just as God is.

God has not demanded an act from you to show your love for Him. You are to experience His love and respond to His love, and the way that is done is by acknowledging the expression of His love in the GOSPEL: Christ and Him crucified.

Many are always looking for what to do to please God, but take a close look at the scripture below:

> "Brethren, my heart's desire and prayer to God for Israel is that they might be saved. (from their religious works, that is,

> man's idea of what pleases God) For I bear them record that they have a zeal of God, but not according to knowledge. For they, being ignorant of God's righteousness and going about to establish their own righteousness, have not submitted themselves unto the righteousness of God. For Christ is the end of the law for righteousness to everyone that believeth" (Romans 10:1-4).

As righteous as the law of Moses was, in the light of the righteousness of God revealed in Christ, the law of Moses is considered as works of the flesh.

The last verse of the scripture above states that Christ is the end of the law of Moses. In the light of the righteousness of God revealed in Christ, God is no longer pleased with all the requirements of the LAW of Moses. We all need to understand that. It is UNLAWFUL to practice the requirements of the LAW of Moses under the priestly ministry of Christ.

All that is required for life and godliness is already contained within the God-life that you became at New birth, and it is called The Law of the Spirit of Life.

> "That the communication of thy faith may become effectual by the acknowledging of EVERY GOOD THING WHICH IS IN YOU IN CHRIST JESUS" (Philemon 1:6).

The new birth is the revealing of the visible image of the invisible God in a man's structural formation.

That was what all creation, both the living and the dead, witnessed when Jesus was justified in the spirit right in hell.

> *"And without controversy great is the mystery of godliness: God was manifest in the flesh, justified in the Spirit, seen of angels, preached unto the Gentiles, believed on in the world, received up into glory" (1 Timothy 3:16).*

His justification was also His resurrection. Resurrection is not a journey out of the grave, no! That is not what it is.

Resurrection is the transition from the state of mortality into immortality. Jesus Christ is the first man to experience God's resurrection power. This transition or resurrection of Jesus Christ took place in hell. Resurrection means the Immortal, uncreated LIFE ESSENCE -God- revealed in Man's structure. I am resurrection and Life. You are resurrection and life. Our Immortal identity is resurrection and life.

CHAPTER 8

The Perfect Law Of Liberty

The new man Christ is a being that transcends time. His memory capacity is God. By the grace of our Lord Jesus Christ, He has inherited the experiences of God beyond time and beyond every beginning of every creation. He can understand every secret of created beings. He can walk back and forth through every beginning because He is highly exalted in God as Creator. He is Alpha and Omega, the immortal man who embodies all realms and dimensions. He is the Lord of creation.

The new creation is uncreated light. He is far above the heavens and beyond every beginning. His ancientness transcends eternity. He is, by birth and by Christ, a member of the Godhead. He is a bearer of the record of God before creation was brought forth.

He is not an ordinary being. Glory!

> "He that believeth on the Son of God hath the witness in himself: he that believeth not God hath made him a liar; because he believeth not the record that God gave of his Son. And this is the record, that God hath given to us eternal life, and this life is in his Son" (1 John 5:10-11 KJV).

There is within your being the record and testimony of God. That record is the experience of God. Just as children inherit their parents' experiences through DNA transmission, a child begins to exhibit certain traits of their father. Likewise, your spirit identity contains the experiences of God, which are willed to the new man.

What God has given to us is beyond good character. He gave us a nature that bears a record and a witness to the life that brought forth eternity, a life that holds the hidden wisdom and secrets of God, the immortality of one who made everything. The implication is that the new creation is more ancient than the creation itself. He is at the beginning of God. He has a nature that can interact with the naked glory of Yahweh, such that the memories of God's experiences are registered in his soul.

> *"Father, I will that they also, whom thou hast given me, be with me where I am; that they may behold my glory, which thou hast given me: for thou lovedst me BEFORE the foundation of the world" (John 17:24, KJV).*

Yes, the new creation is before creation. He is immortality. He is more ancient than the twenty-four elders and other beings. His memory and experiences are not the things that happen to him in time, even though they appear so because of an Adamic consciousness. His memory capacity is that which was from the beginning. He is not time-bound. He is the timeless immortal.

The Bliss Of Immortality

The new creation man is not a being bound by his experiences in time. He is a being exploring the experiences of God beyond beginnings. He is far above the limitations of human experiences.

In other words, it is essential to say that your memory is Christ in the new immortal Identity. Nothing other than the workings of Christ is contained in the memory of your new beginning. Anything that causes us to function below this reality is a fallen influence aimed at preserving the human consciousness intact.

The memory of God within us completely detaches us from the influences and limitations of earthly attachments, creating our experiences according to the reality of the Divine soul. The only remembrance and memory the Lord wants us to have is that which was from the beginning. Our interactions with the light of His face superimpose the Divine Mind against the carnal mind.

The divine soul has no record of the wrongs that people do. It does not have a record of death nor fellowship with the unfruitful works of darkness. God is our memory. So we engage and re-engage life, touch and retouch places of encounters with God, and collect and recollect light.

We will not remain in the human consciousness that uses memory to recollect and reexperience offence, pain, and death. That is fellowshipping with death.

> *"For to be carnally minded is death, but to be spiritually minded is life and peace" (Romans 8:6, KJV).*

If you retain the memory of death, it finds expression in your body: sickness, disease, physical death, and ageing.

The memory of death is every experience you have had that undermines your divinity and celebrates mortality. It is a human reality, registered in the heart, that exalts itself above the reality of God's finished work. As we reflect on the memories of our lives, they find expression in our bodies.

> *"My son, attend to my words; incline thine ear unto my sayings. [22] For they are life unto those that find them and health to all their flesh"* (Proverbs 4:20,22, KJV).

Whatsoever Things Are Pure, Think On These Things

> *"Finally, brethren, whatsoever things are true, whatsoever things are honest, whatsoever things are just, whatsoever things are pure, whatsoever things are lovely, whatsoever things are of good report; if there be any virtue, and if there be any praise, think on these things"* (Philippians 4:8, KJV).

When your experiences and interactions with God are stored in your memory, and as you open up your soul to the light of His glory, and when you nourish your thought realm with the light of life, it directly affects your body.

The Light of His Glory

The glory of God is not one thing you want to press into all by yourself without acknowledging and holding in view God's FINISHED WORK.

Neither is it one remarkable manifestation of power that you will not have the knowledge and understanding of its operations. No. Sons understand the operations of God's glory because they have fellowshipped with the knowledge of glory. Yes, it is our inheritance to understand the operations of our glory.

The knowledge of God's glory cannot be separated from God's glory. It conveys the Person of God, who is the glory. Glory is not cloud or smoke. It is not an overwhelming presence that envelopes you and makes you experience the supernatural. All these are the fruits that glory produces. Glory is the essence of that uncreated Being called God.

- Glory is a mystery
- Glory is the express image of God
- Glory is Immortal Life encoded in Light

Every being created by God wears a dimension of brightness because of the mystery with which they were fashioned. That mystery defines their operation, which is also their name or identity. It is that identity that is responsible for the brightness they exude. Yet they are not in touch with the glory of Yahweh.

We like to see smoke, fire and brightness. We pursue supernatural manifestations, but we don't want to sit under the mighty hand of God, waiting for Him to build us with His revelations. We don't want to endure the classroom experience.

What is a classroom? It is the place in you, in Him, where you gaze into the mysteries of IMMORTALITY. His dealings with you are measured by the light you access.

> *"FATHER, I WILL THAT THEY ALSO, WHOM THOU HAST GIVEN ME, BE WITH ME WHERE I AM; THAT THEY MAY BEHOLD MY GLORY, WHICH THOU HAST GIVEN ME" (John 17:24).*

Glory does not just manifest in isolation. Through interactions, it is first REVEALED and ABSORBED AS CONSCIOUSNESS because glory is the IMAGE and PERSON of the Immortal God.

Intimacy with God is not saying romantic words to Jesus; don't be deceived. Intimacy with Jesus is the divine union. You can never come closer than you already are. He did not bring you near. He brought you in and made you his. You are in, and you are Him. It is the mystery of you in Him and Him in you. When the mysteries of this reality, immortality, are being constructed into your soul region through your spirit's interactions with the Glory of God, you are fellowshipping with immortality.

You in me, I in you. When you come to know in experience, the things Jesus holds and stewards in light are unapproachable, but when you become a fellow steward of light in the Kingdom of this dear Son via a continued increase in stature, how can death touch such a man?

CHAPTER 9

The Anointing

Jesus is the first man to be anointed with the Holy Ghost. He was the Word made flesh, unlike the first Adam, whom God created as a man.

> "How God anointed Jesus of Nazareth with the Holy Ghost and with power: who went about doing good and healing all that were oppressed of the devil; for God was with him" (Acts 10:38).

The Scripture says in Hebrews that Christ, in His state as the New Creation, was anointed with the oil of gladness.

> "Thou hast loved righteousness, and hated iniquity; therefore God, even thy God, hath anointed thee with the oil of gladness above thy fellows." (Hebrews 1:9, KJV).

That oil of gladness is not anointing oil as in the Old Testament or what men use today. It is the fullness of God dwelling in a man's body. Anointing does not come upon a saint from without; it is the Life of Immortality within the saints.

> *"But the anointing which ye have received of him abideth in you"* (1 John 2: 27).

We can see from the scripture 1 John 2: 27, quoted above that the anointing is the life of the saints, not something that comes upon them from the outside.

The exact knowledge of our immortal spirit is required to operate the anointing within us, which is expected to overwhelm the saints from the inside out.

> *"For this is good and acceptable in the sight of God our Saviour, Who will have all men to be saved and to come unto the knowledge of the truth"* (1 Timothy 2:3-4).

The scripture here says that it pleases God our Saviour, who will have all men saved and come to the knowledge of the truth. Why will God desire those who are already saved to come to the knowledge of the truth?

The reason is that knowledge of our spiritual identity is required in our heart and mind to activate Immortal Life in our spirit. The scripture says that Jesus grew in stature. The word "stature" means the knowledge of one's reality (the Anointed Immortal Life). This knowledge is needed in our hearts and minds. That is what is called the renewing of the mind.

What Is Anointing?

- Anointing is not oil in a bottle
- Anointing is not anything liquid
- Anointing is not a sensational feeling

ANOINTING IS LIFE!

Anointing is an English word used to capture the operation of the Godlife or Godhead in the person of the Holy Ghost.

- Anointing is who God is
- Anointing is what we are
- Anointing is who the Holy Ghost is
- Anointing is who the Word of God is
- Anointing is the uncreated LIFE of Divinity

We do not mean three distinct personalities when we say God, Ghost, and Word. The Godhead is one personality and not three. The personality of the Godhead is the spirit personality of the saint (the new creation man). Anointing is, in reality, a state of being in Immortality. Anyone born of the Immortal God is anointed with the Holy Ghost and power.

In the Old Testament dispensation, God provided specific instructions for preparing a special physical oil called the anointing oil. The ointment contained many things in one. It was used for consecration. That mixture was poured upon kings and priests as a sign of separation for Yahweh. This oil is a shadow of the real substance of the Immortal personality called the Holy Ghost. The real anointing is a personality. He operates in and through the living.

The physical oil was used to anoint the spiritually dead Israel, but the person of the Holy Ghost is used to anoint the living under the New Testament dispensation.

The anointing (Ghost of God) is a teacher. He teaches and instructs in righteousness. By Him, we know all things. The anointing is the essence, the life of God operating in the believer.

Don't go looking for what you already are in a bottle. It is an insult to the Godhead to say that their essence (Anointing) is in a bottle. The Anointing of God can only inhabit the Living.

That is not to say that power cannot be transferred into substances for healing purposes, but it is important to know that you are the anointing that flowed into the bottle. Therefore, you are greater than the bottle. Yes, life's substance or power can be transferred to persons, objects, and materials, but God only inhabits the living.

What was given to Israel was not the anointing but a shadow of it. Did they experience God? Yes, but they did not receive the promise of God inhabiting a man.

Civilisation is a culture weaved by the governing light in a sphere. So, when you hear 'civilisation,' you are referring to the kind of light and enlightenment that exists within a dimension.

Human civilisation, as seen today, is a demotion into death. Civilisation springs from life and continues to evolve. Celestial beings do not grow old. Why? They operate in a civilisation that forbids them from any form of depreciation.

The civilisation of the fallen man is driven by a kind of light: death. That is why there is nothing new under the sun. Everything under the influence of corruption is old, ageing, depreciating and decomposing. They have good appearances, plus many advantages, but with a sting in the tail. Man has never created anything that was not harmful to him. Why? It is all a flow from his being. Death begets corruption.

The evil in human civilisation is that it attempts to ameliorate the effects of sin and death: build comfort for men that would generate pseudo-pleasure amid spiritual decay and decadence. The idea is that men should be at ease with sin and death. So they wither and wrinkle under the weight and bondage of corruption without ever realizing their need for God.

The Civilization Called "Truth"

> *"To this end was I born, and for this cause came I into the world, that I should bear witness unto the truth. Everyone that is of the truth heareth my voice" (John 18:37).*

There is a civilisation that excels, the civilisation whose origin is God. This civilisation transcends anything in the celestial world. By civilisation, I mean a particular way of life. A culture in God that far supersedes any other in creation. God's life is far above the heavens. It is in this civilisation that you and I reside. This is the civilisation revealed in Christ Jesus after He condemned sin in the flesh and abolished death.

This Civilisation Is Called Life And Immortality

> *"Who hath saved us, and called us with a holy calling, not according to our works, but according to his own purpose and grace, which was given us in Christ Jesus before the world began, But is now made manifest by the appearing of our Saviour Jesus Christ, who hath abolished death, and hath brought life and immortality to light through the gospel" (2 Timothy 1:9-10).*

Life and Immortality are both the nature and character of God. His Civilisation springs from His life, a life that births and sustains all things, incorruptible. We are born of the incorruptible seed. Christ. Christ is the way, the truth, the life, the civilisation itself.

In this civilisation, man is absorbed into Divinity. Man is God. A man takes on the nature, heart, soul, and body of God. The blood has made this possible.

Therefore, if any man is in Christ, he is a new creature. New speaks of that which springs from the foreverness of God. Newness is a culture in God that is replete in all creation. It is the signature of Life. Everything in creation that has life, in its glory estate, breathes freshness.

God has a culture - Immortality. God is life. The character of God's civilisation is NEWNESS. His power that upholds all things keeps creation in life. Life is a signature of glory. Living is the culture of glory. Glory loves. Glory evolves. Glory lives. Glory radiates and emits a love flame. Glory is the effulgence of life. So everything that has not fallen from its glory estate is alive and bears a kind of living light by which it is kept. This is love.

The civilisation of God is far above the dimensions of creation. Of His will, Man was born into this height of nobility. Therefore, man is admitted into the fellowship of ONE. GOD is the mystery of ONE.

Out of the two (Jews and Gentiles), God has made one new man. We are Christ the New Man. If any man is in God, he is in the fellowship of ONE. A dimension where all are absorbed into ONE. God. John said, 'I saw One sitting on the throne. Indeed, that ONE is many.

The God-Man is born to think God - thoughts. He is to hold divine thoughts and envision and imagine as God. He is to desire as God desires. He is to will as God because He is born of the will of God. He has the mind of Christ, which is the intelligence of immortality.

He is face to face with the God of Glory. He is to interact with the light upon the face of Jesus Christ. The very light of the world to be revealed in us is Christ, who is our world. Building up a saint with anything other than this truth is wrong and impossible.

When we speak of the world to come, we are not talking about something far away in the future. We are talking of a reality in us coming forth to find expression. That world is within us. The kingdom is within us. The power and glory are within us. We are the future.

The World To Come Is Now

The world to come appears from within us. It is not coming sometime in the future because it is NOW. It is coming from within us. Christ in us is that world to manifest!

Every truth being unveiled, every insight being given, every dealing and instruction being dished out to us by the Spirit of truth is all for one purpose: to make us embodiments of the knowledge of love that passes knowledge. Creation will be delivered when the sons of love arise. This is the mark of the Saviours arising in Zion. Pure love is the living expression of heaven's civilisation.

The one who was, who is, who is to come is the one who transcends time and eternity. He has introduced us to that transcendent life by the gospel, and as we begin to melt this world (corruption) with the fervent heat of the life of Christ, we know that the civilisation of Life is invading the Kingdom of this world.

When perspectives begin to shift from human thoughts to God's thoughts; when the light by which men see changes from the light of death to the light of life; when men become increasingly overwhelmed by a bottomless desire for the living water, and their desperation drives them to drink God fountains flowing all over the earth, when the love of Christ has so intoxicated the sons that everything in creation comes under the power of the love that we emit, then Isaiah 2 is being fulfilled.

Creation shall weep no more. The gospel shall be preached to every creature. Yes, unveiling God's civilisation will deliver the creature from the bondage of corruption. This is achievable as we commit to interacting with the light of God's glory, as revealed in the face of Jesus Christ. Out of that face proceedeth the light of our civilisation. The Bible says these things shall be in our time. Amen.

He Who Was Who Is And Is To Come

The coming of God reveals His civilisation from within. It is the new creation-man: Christ and His priests.1 Cor 15:23. The earth shall be filled with the knowledge of the glory of the Lord as the waters cover the sea. But every man in his own order: Christ the firstfruits; afterwards they that are Christ's at his coming.

Christ is our culture. He is our way of life. He is the life that we are. We are committed to exploring this reality and consistently pushing through the veils in our hearts, shredding them into pieces at the entrances of our light and our world. The Lamb is that light. He is the light by which we live. He is our world.

The Anointing

Reflection Point

Personal Notes:

―――――― Guided Action Plan ――――――

CHAPTER 10

Revelation Knowledge

"That which was from the beginning, which we have heard, which we have seen with our eyes, which we have looked upon, and our hands have handled, of the Word of life. (For the life was manifested, and we have seen it, and bear witness, and shew unto you that eternal life, which was with the Father, and was manifested unto us;) That which we have seen and heard declare we unto you, that ye also may have fellowship with us: and truly our fellowship is with the Father, and with his Son Jesus Christ"(1 John 1:1-3).

God is Spirit. You relate to Him with your spirit. Those who worship Him do so in spirit and truth. Those who see Him do so in spirit and truth. Those who look upon Him do so with their spirit eyes. Understanding is the eyes of the spirit man. So, to see God is beyond seeing His form; it is coming into interaction with the very essence of His being. It is perilous or, say, IMPOSSIBLE for anything not born of Him.

Now God is light, and so is everyone born of Him. Your light and the light that God is ARE THE SAME because you are born of Him. You have His DNA. His Word is His DNA.

> "Of his own will begat he us with the word of truth, that we should be a kind of firstfruits of his creatures" (James 1:18).

You are born not of blood, the will of man, the will of the flesh, but of God. The very seed of God is in you. You can see Him. To see God is not to see him in a vision. There is nothing wrong with that level of seeing, but seeing a vision of God does not mean you have seen Him.

The highest encounter with God is for a saint to gain spiritual understanding of who God is.

> "And this is life eternal, that they might know thee the only true God, and Jesus Christ, whom thou hast sent" (John 17:3).

When a man sees God in this way, he not only gains knowledge about God but also becomes an embodiment of that dimension of God that he has seen and stewards that God dimension.

You cannot separate God from the believer. But a believer unaware of His oneness with God will live in defeat, like a mere man. God forbid!

> "They know not, neither will they understand; they walk on in darkness: all the foundations of the earth are out of course. I have said, Ye are gods, and all of you are children of the Most High. But ye shall die like men and fall like one of the princes" (Psalm 82:5-7).

So, seeing God is coming into the spiritual understanding of who He is and what He contains. To know God experientially is to know what God knows. It is to come to awareness and embodiment of the knowledge He keeps as God. No celestial being or prophet of old functioned at that level of sight. They saw things about God, but their entrance into those things was withheld because Christ had not yet been revealed! Christ is man's access to the immortal realms.

Isaiah had a vision of the Lord. He saw the Lord upon the throne, but the truth is that Isaiah did not see God. He had a prophetic experience and was caught up to see the activities in heaven. He saw a form of God sitting on the throne. But he did not see God. No man born in the similitude of fallen Adam can see God outside Christ. Christ is the mirror that reflects God.

As a living soul, Adam was meant to feed on the Tree of Life, which could have allowed him to see God, as he had an ordination to transition from man to Godman. Adam's course was truncated, and access to the Tree of Life was denied. The pure spirit nature that enabled him to interact with God was lost.

Ezekiel had a powerful experience with God. He saw a form of being sitting upon the throne. Did he see right? Yes. Did he see God? No. To see God means to UNDERSTAND who He is, what he is, and what He is made up of and to embody it. To embody means to wear or put on that garment of Light, the Mind of Christ. That is the crown of wisdom we must put on. It is a body of light or knowledge.

> *'No man hath seen God at any time; the only begotten Son, which is in the bosom of the Father, he hath declared him"* (*John 1:18*).

Jesus said in the scripture above that no man had seen God before except Him alone.

When Moses asked to see God, he did not ask for visions of God. He was asking to understand the mystery of God truly, but that was impossible for a spirit that was dead.

Moses craved a revelation of God's person that would alter him from mortality into immortality. Moses wanted to see the beginning of the Uncreated One. His Self Essence. He wanted to see God's face. God's face is His beginningless beginning - IMMORTALITY. That was too much for a mortal man to ask.

The reason why God told Moses that no man could see Him and live was that Moses was dead in his spirit, and a dead spirit could not comprehend the uncreated God. All of humanity experienced death in Adam before physical birth.

> *"For as in Adam all die, even so in Christ shall all be made alive"* (1 Corinthians 15:22).

Now, when a man truly sees God, the glory light from His being shoots into such a man, and either of two things would happen: either you contain the effulgence of that glory light and become an embodiment of it, or you cease to be. For the dead, it would mean an end to existence. For the immortal ones, it is a symbol of eternal glory.

The Bliss Of Immortality

> "But we all, with open face beholding as in a glass the glory of the Lord, are changed into the same image from glory to glory, even as by the Spirit of the Lord" (2 Corinthians 3:18).

The new creation man can contain God's effulgence and embody that glory light (knowledge), but a mortal spirit cannot, not even celestial beings. That is why God said to Moses, "I will show you my back". The back God showed Moses was the face of His creation (eternity), THE BEGINNING OF CREATION. Moses became an embodiment of reality in God as a result of that experience of seeing.

What Moses saw was not just a form of God. He saw into the mysteries of God in creation. He came into the custodianship of a reality of God in eternity. He did not just see a form; he saw a person. He touched substance and essence. That is what it means to SEE—no wonder he did not age.

> "And Moses was a hundred and twenty years old when he died: his eye was not dim, nor his natural force abated" (Deuteronomy 34:7).

He saw into a secret that reversed the operation of death in his body. Moses' experience with God's back opened the beginning of creation to him. He was taken back in time, not in a vision, but in an actual time travel experience. He went back in time to see what transpired in creation before and after the fall of man.

Imagine Moses in the Old Testament, which is not even glorious compared to the Testament of life that we bear in Christ.

Containing The Light

> "O righteous Father, the world hath not known thee: but I have known thee....." (John 17:25).

What Jesus is saying, in other words, is that the world cannot see you, Father, but I can see you, and the things I do are what I see you do. Hallelujah!

> "And we know that the Son of God is come, and hath given us an understanding, that we may know him that is true" (1 John 5:20).

We are given AN UNDERSTANDING (sight) that we might know Him who is TRUE. Without understanding, no one can claim to have seen the Lord. You may have seen Him in a vision without actually coming into the revelation of His person and becoming the embodiment of that revealed truth. To embody a dimension of truth (God) means establishing that truth in your soul through your spirit's interactions.

Back To 1 John Chapter One

> "That which was from the beginning, which we have heard, which we have seen with our eyes, which we have looked upon, and our hands have handled, of the Word of life; (For the life was manifested, and we have seen it, and bear witness, and shew unto you that eternal life, which was with the Father and was manifested unto us;). That which we have seen and heard declare we unto you, that ye also may have fellowship with us: and truly our fellowship is with the Father and with his Son Jesus Christ" (1 John 1:1-3).

The Bliss Of Immortality

John 1 John 5:20 speaks of that which was from the beginning. The beginning John is talking about here is not the beginning of creation. It was the beginning when it was only GOD. God is that which was from the beginning. John tells us that He has seen that Being, heard that Being, looked upon (fixed his eyes), and touched and handled that Being, who is from the beginning.

This is the same Being who could not reveal Himself to Moses. What is the difference? Spirit nature.

Spirits are light. A spirit created by GOD has a kind of glorious light, which is very beautiful and adorable. People see angels and are wowed by their beauty and majesty. But the New Creation is a superior breed. He is a spirit born of the exact light of the Uncreated One. Celestial beings marvel at our kind of light because it is not like anything ever seen or known before. That light is the dominion by which creation will be delivered.

> *"Of his own will begat he us by the word of truth" (James 1:18).*

The new man is compatible with God's glorious realms (glory-realm) because of His peculiar spirit and light nature. This is the reason why he is a wonder to the angelic world. Yes, you! I mean you! You are a wonder to the 24 elders and the seraphim. They admire you. They desire to look into the things of which you are made, but it is not given to them to see. It is through you that they will ever be able to understand God.

> "To the intent that now unto the principalities and powers in heavenly places might be known by the church the manifold wisdom of God" (Ephesians 3:10).

The principalities and powers here are not evil spirits. They are celestial beings of glory who will be taught by the saints God's manifold wisdom hidden in the ages. They will be released into greater manifestations of glory in their order as the saints unveil the manifold faces of God to them.

This is what it means to judge angels. It means we would illuminate them. They, too, are part of the creation and are waiting for our manifestation. The saints will judge angels because they are born of a superior spirit, a light essence.

We (our spirit personality) are the glory of God revealed in a visible image form, and we see God by revelation and interaction with His face in us. The revelation of God with which we interact is forbidden to angels and other celestial beings. They cannot see Him because they do not have the spiritual capacity to contain him, but we are spirits made of light, unapproachable. We behold, and then we show forth.

> "But ye are a chosen generation, a royal priesthood, a holy nation, a peculiar people; that ye should show forth the praises of him who hath called you out of darkness into his marvellous light" (1 Peter 2:9).

Blessed be the Lord God Almighty. Which was. Which is and which is to come. The Almighty!

CHAPTER 11

The Womb Of Immortality

> *"The Holy Spirit this signifying that the way into the Holiest of all was not yet made manifest, while as the first tabernacle was yet standing..." (Hebrews 9:8).*

The Holiest of all is the place where God dwells in light unapproachable. It is the separation of God into which the saint is admitted by new birth.

It is the Womb of the Morning, where every other morning or beginning was birthed. This is where the saint is right now. He might not have received the experiential knowledge of this place; he might not be aware of the reality of this place. He might even be living a sense-ruled life, but that does not change the reality that the saint is NOW present in the Holiest of all by the blood of Jesus Christ (His life).

The saint does not journey into God's presence. He is born there. He lives there. He is God's home. The believer embodies the presence of God because the believer is Christ. We were all baptised into Christ, the brightness of God's glory and the exact representation of His person. That man Christ is us, and we are Him. For such a High Priest became us who is holy, harmless, undefiled, separate from sinners, and made higher than the heavens. He became us, and we became Him.

Therefore, it is necessary to mention that the saint is responsible for keeping his mind focused on fellowship with his realm. Christ is your realm. If you are then risen with Christ, your culture as the kingdom man is to set your mind and your affection upon the right-hand side where you (Christ) are seated

We need to grow and mature in our consciousness of where we are and move from place to place, from realm to realm, in the place where we are born.

We need to take off the former conversation (thought lines and formations, imaginative structures, emotional patterns) and take on the soul of Christ.

As we grow in consciousness of who we are and where we are, we expose our hearts to the light of our current location. We grow in our identity consciousness and function as sons.

Our journey is to know that we are in the Father, with the Father in the Holiest of all. Understanding this reality changes our attitude and our walk. You function from rest and victory.

The new person needs to interact with their new reality and experience the heavenly places in Christ Jesus through communion with truth. He who communes with the truth can submit to and be governed by truth.

> *"The Lord himself is our Tabernacle; in Him, all veils are taken away for our sake" (Heb 9:11).*

In Christ, God has stripped Himself naked and made the invisible God visible and crystal clear to us, in us, and through us. Where veils exist is in the unrenewed mind of the saint, which is why there is a need to expose the soul to the truth. Truth shatters veils. The revelation of Jesus shines upon the heart, bringing illumination and removing the veils.

The structure of the Tabernacle that Moses built was a form of entrance for the spiritually dead Jews to access God's presence. The Tabernacle consisted of three courts: the outer court, the Holy Place, and the Most Holy Place. Why? Because the people of that first covenant were dead in their spirit, which was why the Tabernacle was constructed for them. They were to journey from the outer court into the holy and most holy places. The High Priest embarked on that journey on behalf of all of Israel because the people could not approach God.

The New Testament Tabernacle bears no resemblance to the Tabernacle in the Old Testament. This tabernacle, which is Christ, does not have veils like the one Moses had. David's open-face Tabernacle captures this well.

God clothes Himself with lights, and to the New Creation man, the lights of God are an invitation to him for adventures at the heights and depths of Divinity because he is naturally compatible with that light.

The Tabernacle of God has many heavenly places. The New Creation man's journey is one of discovering who he is and experiencing the heavenly places in Christ Jesus. We do not know how many there are, but we know they are MANY. So he journeys from place to place, in the Holiest of all, and from where He is. We are in God exploring the fullness we have received, grace for grace.

Under the first covenant, the priest journeyed from outside into the inner courts. But we were born right in the HOLIEST OF ALL and are still in the Holiest of all. We are born of the light that is called "unapproachable."

Our journey and our movement are from the very inside of God. It is an indication of how we live. We live from the inside out. In the olden times, they observed ceremonial rituals and washings that sanctified them outwardly.

But our life is lived from within because we have been sanctified.

We are Ekklesia! We worship the Father as Life-giving Spirits born of the incorruptible sperm of God, which liveth and abideth forever. We are the ones who worship Him in spirit, and in truth, our souls and bodies are being flooded with the light that we are from the inside out.

We do not press into the Holiest of all. We journey into experiences in our Father from the Holiest of all. We discover heavenly places in Christ and function from there. This place(s) is a person. In Him, we live. In Him, we move. In Him, we have our being. We are not pressing into Him. We are in Him, looking into Him, learning Him and discovering Him.

CHAPTER 12

A New Consciousness

It is not doing that makes us become. We do because we are. Who we are is our blessing, and the manifestation of our being will flow from this place of immortal self-realisation. You do not do things to become anything in Christ; you receive the knowledge of who Christ has made you in Himself and register that knowledge in your heart and mind through fellowship. You receive the Father's dealings with you due to the knowledge of truth He has exposed you to.

That knowledge awakens in you the consciousness of your immortal identity. Your receiving the knowledge of the Son of God, your intentional response to the Father in submitting to the lordship of the revealed truth, authorises your functioning at the level of light you have interacted with and authorises you to function as who you already are. So you understand that your response to truth is helping you (not God) to express and manifest what you were freely given.

All dimensions in Christ Jesus are A FREE GIFT. However, we grow up operating in them. We learn by beholding. Our learning is not for becoming but for discovering the new self, understanding the inheritance, mastering righteousness, kingdom functionality, and taking responsibility for what is already given.

You function as a son and produce the fruit of righteousness because you yield to grace for growth, understanding, and mastery of what was freely given.

Understanding your being, tattooed in your soul by your interaction with light, enables you to function as the new you. You don't manifest your being without knowing you are registered in your heart. That knowledge is intercourse with light that takes out the old mind and heart and brings your consciousness into your actual reality, Christ.

Hold Your Reality In View

The casual seeker finds God on the surface, but the diligent seeker finds God from depth to depth. He keeps moving in the light until He touches the very ENTITY projecting that light until he sees with precision, clarity and accuracy.

This is the difference between the little children and the young men/fathers (all of them are sons at different levels, please). Clarity in sight and understanding differentiates between the various levels of maturity.

A diligent seeker drinks the water of light until it overflows from his within and becomes wearing, covering: consciousness superimposed on every contrary experience. In this manner, mortality will be swallowed up by immortality.

You will dance a strange dance when your heart is full of wine. You will take steps ordered in the light of truth. Truth is not a commandment; He is a being to be loved and fellowshipped with. He is a reality with which to interact. Truth is a person to be known and to be enjoyed. But the key to experiencing this is fellowship.

This is the Father's emphasis in this season: sons who are drunk with the revelation of Christ, who not only understand that they are the righteousness of God in Christ Jesus, but who also take up the responsibility of reigning as the righteousness of God in Christ Jesus. God wants the righteous ones to REIGN in righteousness. Our responsibility as the righteous ones is to REIGN. Light reigns.

The Mind Of Christ

Darkness and gross darkness can only flee by the operation of immortality in the order of light (understanding).

In His living soul, Jesus had an understanding of his IMMORTAL IDENTITY. He could refer to Himself as the "I AM," a word used to capture an uncreated LIFE ESSENCE. The Jews said He was not even up to 50, but He replied that He was before Abraham. John declared, 'He is before me'. There was something

John knew about this mystery man. He was too much of a puzzle to be solved by mortal brains.

> *"Let this MIND be in you, which was also in Christ Jesus: Who, being in the form of God, thought it not robbery to be equal with God" (Philippians 2:5-6).*

He functioned with a mind clothed with an identity that offended the people He was sent to. The scriptures say that His own did not know Him. They could not receive Him.

There was a mind with which He functioned. That was the MIND, which was said to be in Christ. Jesus is a body of light, the knowledge of His immortal identity, and all His experiences as the immortal God, which He set aside to be made flesh. The scripture instructs us to allow that same mind to be in us. This is about a posture that made Him humble Himself in obedience to death. Also, that attitude or posture enabled Him to submit Himself to be taught the knowledge of the Life that He was as the Immortal Deity.

His immortal glory, the joy set before Him, enabled Him to endure the cross and despise the shame. That joy was not that He was going back to the Father. That joy was that humanity was coming to possess that same immortal Identity exclusive to the Godhead, such that the presence of the Man, Jesus Christ, becomes the presence of all humanity who believe in the immortal Godhead.

This understanding is the knowledge of the Immortal identity of Jesus, the knowledge of Him in the form of God. It was required for Him to know Himself as the Lord God, even in His form as a man. His growth in stature was marked by his acquisition of knowledge about his Divine nature. He was not born with that knowledge physically. He acquired it here on earth. It became His consciousness. His acts, utterances, and responses came from that consciousness.

"Thou hast made known to me the ways of life" (Acts 2:28).

A Crown Consciousness

God met Moses in the desert and said, "See, I have made you God to Pharaoh!" The word 'see' is so relevant here. Moses was to hold in view the consciousness of whom God said He made him. That consciousness would be worn like a crown around his head and mind. That was his authority over the Egyptian gods.

There is no darkness, no matter how thick, our Immortal identity's mind (understanding) cannot dislodge. There is no disease or sickness the mind of Christ cannot terminate. To have the mind of Christ is to have the functional knowledge of the "Christyou". This is the knowledge that displaces every high thing that exalts itself against the knowledge of God and brings every thought into the obedience of Christ.

The saint is God to every spirit, whether created, dead, or alive. We must learn to hold in view the understanding of our **IMMORTAL IDENTITY**; that is the highest form of prayer.

Creation will influence you if you do not know that you are God. Therefore, wake up! We are to govern the creation and declare God's manifold wisdom to principalities and powers in the heavenly places. Ruling and reigning require a clear-cut understanding of Christ.

Take A Careful Look At This Scripture Below

> *"For God, who commanded the light to shine out of darkness, hath shone in our hearts, to give the light of the knowledge of the glory of God in the face of Jesus Christ. But we have this treasure in earthen vessels, that the excellency of the power may be of God, and not of us" (2 Corinthians 4:6-7).*

This scripture clearly states that we have this treasure in our earthen vessel. The treasure here is our IMMORTALITY. That treasure is our spirit personality. This personality is what is called in Hebrews 1:3: the brightness of God's glory and the express image of His person. Do you see who you are? Glory!

The knowledge of this treasure which we are, which is in this our earthen vessel, is what God, who commanded the light to shine out of darkness, is giving to us now according to this same scripture. The knowledge is STATURE, while the treasure is our NATURE.

I know who I am.

CHAPTER 13

Aerodynamic Law And The Law Of The Spirit Of Life

Today, we all fly aeroplanes. We have forgotten that there was a time when no man, not even the wisest among men, could imagine a massive object like a plane flying in the air. Man's interactions with a kind of knowledge made that miracle possible for all men.

You will appreciate what I just said better when you are shown the weight of some aeroplanes. What do you think the law of the Spirit of life can do?

> "1Verily, verily, I say unto you, if a man keeps my saying, he shall never see death" (John 8:5).

Jesus, in the scripture above, told us one of the things the law of the spirit of life is capable of doing. What we are to believe are the things the law of the Spirit of Life can do. You notice that the moment Jesus mentioned the issue of not seeing death in the scripture above, the Jews were offended.

Hear What They Said To Jesus

> *"Art thou greater than our father Abraham, which is dead? and the prophets are dead: whom makest thou thyself?" (John 8:53).*

Their response to Jesus is no different from that of most believers today when they hear the truth of life and immortality, yet we are supposed to know better because of our new birth experience. You will also notice that Jesus did not tell them what He said. He couldn't because they were dead men. A man who is spiritually dead cannot comprehend the reality of immortality. The saying of Jesus in the above scripture is the truth, and the truth is immortality. Immortality is the tree Adam was instructed to fellowship with (eat) in Eden before he fell and was sent out of Eden.

That tree was not literal. It was knowledge, the knowledge of the glory of immortality. I am sure you know that death truncated Adam's fellowship with the knowledge of immortality in the Garden of Eden.

The Immortal God became man to remove sin, abolish death and restore the knowledge of immortality for Man to feed on again.

Look At The Scriptures Below

> *"Who, being in the form of God, thought it not robbery to be equal with God: But made himself of no reputation, and took upon him the form of a servant, and was made in the likeness of men. And being found in fashion as a man, he humbled himself and became obedient unto death, even the death of the cross" (Philippians 2:6-8).*

The scripture above says that He was in the form of God. He was not just in the form of God. He was God. But He became man so that He could remove or abolish death and then make the knowledge of immortality available again to man.

> "But now once in the end of the world hath he appeared to put away sin by the sacrifice of himself" (Hebrews 9:2).

The scripture here states that Jesus came at the end of the age to take away sin, which is the root cause of physical death, ageing, sickness, and disease.

The saying of Jesus, which He says will stop a man that keeps it from seeing death, is that which was revealed after death was abolished, and his sacrifice removed sin.

Let's See What It Is In The Scripture Below

> "Who hath saved us, and called us with a holy calling, not according to our works, but according to his own purpose and grace, which was given us in Christ Jesus before the world began, But is now made manifest by the appearing of our Saviour Jesus Christ, who hath abolished death, and hath brought life and immortality to light through the gospel: Whereunto I am appointed a preacher, and an apostle, and a teacher of the Gentiles. (2 Timothy 1:9-11, KJV).

You can see that what God revealed after He abolished death was life and immortality. Apostle Paul said he was made a teacher of it to the Gentiles. The resurrected man is the gospel that reveals truth, life, and immortality. Life and immortality are His name. His name speaks of his identity or spirit personality.

The Scripture Below Bears Witness To It

"Who being the brightness of his glory, and the express image of his person, and upholding all things by the word of his power" (Hebrews 1:3).

Whatever He upholds by the Word of His Power cannot die. How does He uphold? He does that through the light of the knowledge of His glory.

Our high calling is to feed on the knowledge of life and immortality. This knowledge is what God feeds us with.

Look At The Scripture Below

"For God, who commanded the light to shine out of darkness, hath shined in our hearts, to give the light of the knowledge of the glory of God in the face of Jesus Christ" (2 Cor. 4:6).

This knowledge of life and immortality is the saying of Jesus, which the believer must keep to enforce the testimony of life.

A Living Testimony

The life of God in my spirit is the government of God. Everything created is subject to this life.

The man's five senses, which serve as his medium of learning, did not witness the finished work of God because the work was done within his spiritual personality.

No one can comprehend the reality of God's finished work in Christ through the five senses. That is not to say that our physical senses cannot respond to spiritual realities. They were not meant to be limited to physical realities; they are doorways through which a man is accessed.

However, I am saying that at New Birth, your physical senses did not witness the transaction because this body has fallen, and the senses are in a fallen state. It was a purely spirit experience.

That is why Scripture states that spiritual things are discerned spiritually. We can only lay hold of that truth via our spirit.

The word "OLD" is used to capture a spiritually dead state. Satan became old when his spirit died, and Adam also became old. To say I am an old man or I am getting old means to acknowledge that you are a dead spirit who is out of alignment with God.

If the testimony within the ark in the Old Testament fought and conquered nations on behalf of the Israelites, how much more will the life-giving testimony concealed within our spirit, made of the power of an endless life, conquer mortality and corruption in our body? We are immortal spirits operating through an earthen vessel (physical body).

The Life-giving Spirit is the testimony of the power of an endless life. The Immortal Priesthood of Christ was brought forth to preside over this testimony of Life. We are the testimony.

The saints are suffering because they lack knowledge of God's testimony, which informs their relationship with the Father.

The New Testament Law, which is the power of God unto salvation, is the spirit of the new creation of man; this law is the

Life that God is. The knowledge of God's testimony in your heart is the way to conquer physical death, ageing, sickness, and diseases.

Every spirit carries testimony within it, which informs its relationship with its Creator. The new creation man also has his God-given testimony concealed within himself (in his spirit).

Ignoring this New Testament results in being out of fellowship with one's identity. The generation of believers that will conquer physical death, ageing, sickness, and diseases is the one that will free creation from the bondage of corruption. We are emerging!

God's relationship with everything he created is based on the knowledge of his testimony contained within their being. Ignorance of this testimony is darkness. Darkness is the absence of illumination.

The knowledge of the testimony of God in your spirit needs to be in your heart/mind for you to experience the operation of the life of the testimony. That is what it means to put on the new man. To wear the knowledge of that reality as a living consciousness that governs everything we do from the inside out. Lesser realities no longer govern us. We live from the world within, from the highest place, Christ in us!

> *"In Him was life, and the life was the light of men. 5 And the light shines in the darkness, and the darkness did not comprehend it" (John 1:4-5).*

The Bliss Of Immortality

God is light. By Him, all things and all realms of life were created. His light travels through all realms of existence, all eternity and immortality. According to this scripture, this light shines in the darkness. What is referred to as 'darkness' here in this scripture is a twisted, perverted kind of life which came about by the fall of Lucifer. Darkness lives in men who have not received the light of life. The atmosphere of darkness is sponsored by the darkness resident in men's hearts, and it would take the sons of God to drive away such darkness by shining the light on their lives.

Darkness has nothing within it that can understand the manifold wisdom of God. It is not that darkness tried to understand the light but was unable to. It does not have to. Why? It cannot dissect the light which God is. It is not only darkness that lacks the strength to comprehend the light which God is, but this also applies to all that God created. However, because God's creatures are still alive, they possess a kind of living light, so according to their light, they have a comprehension of God because they are alive.

But the new creation which comprehends the fullness of this Light. Why? It is because we are Christ by nature 1Cor 15:23; We are God's righteousness, which all created beings are not. We are begotten sons of the uncreated God. Have you come to terms with this reality about yourself, or are you still holding onto the old man's image in your mind? That is death. Holding to the image of the new man in Christ is life and peace.

> *"Therefore, just as through one man sin entered the world, and death through sin, and thus death spread to all men because all sinned" (Rom 5:12-13, NKJV).*

Satan became darkness because he fell; he wasn't created so. The inability of darkness to comprehend God's light is not because it is darkness, but because it cannot. There is simply no access granted for such interaction to bring about comprehension.

Even before Satan became darkness, his ability to comprehend that light was only in a measure. The glory of God that creatures reflect is the measure of glory that God has given them to express, and that is the extent to which they can comprehend Him. When a creature falls away from Him, it can no longer comprehend Him. It becomes lawless. But the Man Christ is a being without measures. He is the Abundant and the Bountiful One.

The Darkness Of Man
It becomes clear that darkness is the state of the fallen man —the man in his fallen state has become one with Satan (1 Corinthians 6:14). Man cannot comprehend the Light, even though he is still redeemable. The true light lightens every man who comes into the world because man became darkness. It is easier to understand this when we consider David's utterance, *"You will enlighten my darkness"* (Psalms 18:28).

Man's comprehension of God became darkened, so he could no longer comprehend the light. Even when the light manifested Himself among His own, they knew him not. They received Him not because men, being darkness, have loved darkness rather than light.

The light of God shines in every realm. His glory is seen in every plane because His kingdom governs all. His dominion permeates all creation. All dimensions are bare before His eyes. The light of God shines in the darkness, but darkness cannot even see Him.

Because we saints are born in the realm of God's light, we ought not to live in fear. Our understanding of our spiritual position will destroy every fear of Satan, who is in darkness. The fact that our physical body is here on earth does not mean that we are in the same realm as Satan.

This earth is not the realm of darkness, even though the civilisation which Satan brought forth when he took over the lordship of the earth is still running. That is why John said that even though we are in this world system, we are not of the world. We have the light of God. We are not in darkness; let us lay hold of this reality now and walk as sons of God who we are.

> *"And this is the record that God hath given to us eternal life, and this life is in his Son. He that hath the Son hath life, and he that hath not the Son of God hath not life. These things have I written unto you that believe on the name of the Son of God; that ye may know that ye have eternal life and that ye may believe on the name of the Son of God" (1 John 5:11-13).*

Aerodynamic Law And The Law Of The Spirit Of Life

Reflection Point

Personal Notes: _____

Guided Action Plan

CHAPTER 14

Our Immortal Garment

When God made Man, Man needed no physical clothing because he was not naked. He had a supernatural garment. That garment was his spirit man. That spirit of man was not just in the body; it was both an indwelling and an outward overwhelming of the body. That was the clothing of the body of Man.

In the beginning, the spirit man was both within and upon the body. The body of Man was kept inside him, the spirit. The spirit was the house that carried the body and sustained it. That was the technology of a living soul's life. That was why that first man needed no clothes, no vehicles or planes, no kitchen to cook food. He was a Superman. His state in life placed him above all that was created. He was God over the works of God's hands.

His body could neither age nor wrinkle because the life he was overwhelmed the body from within and formed a shield for it. He was a man with a lit body. His body was bread. His body was without leaven!

But as soon as he fell, the body became the house of his spirit, which is the other way around now. The spirit died and caved into the body. The man suddenly became naked, needing clothes made from creation to cover himself. He was meant to cover creation, but He was found naked.

He could no longer function as God of the earth because wearing a heavenly spirit nature was the 'mantle' or sceptre by which he ruled. He was a living soul-spirit man whose presence sustained all creation and kept them alive. Adam was the covering of God over creation. He was the presence of God upon the earth. He was the Chief Priest, and His garment sprouted from His being, not externally.

> *"For we know that if our earthly house of this tabernacle were dissolved, we have a building of God, a house not made with hands, eternal in the heavens. For in this, we groan, earnestly desiring to be clothed upon with our house which is from heaven: If so be that being clothed we shall not be found naked. For we that are in this tabernacle do groan, being burdened: not for that we would be unclothed, but clothed upon, that mortality might be swallowed up of life"* (2 Corinthians 5:1-4).

Your Spirit is your heaven because your Spirit is Christ. Christ is your heaven. Spirits wear their habitation as a garment. Remember that God our Father is clothed with light as a garment and dwells in the light that no man (created spirits) can approach. So His dwelling and His garment are one.

Take a close look at his prayer in the scripture below,

> *"And now, O FATHER, GLORIFY thou ME with THINE OWN SELF with the GLORY which I HAD with THEE before the world was" (John 17:5).*

To glorify is to be clothed with, to cover with, to immerse with. Glory IS LIFE ESSENCE; it speaks of the spirit personality, which is not separate from the body and the soul, like the fallen man whose three parts are disjointed because of corruption.

All three are enveloped as a being. This is what it means to be whole. To be bread. When the entire being has only one testimony in all its faculties, Spirit, soul and body were not meant to be divided. They are one indivisible whole.

The Lord Jesus Christ, in His prayer, was telling the Father to clothe Him with His Spirit personality. That prayer was answered at His resurrection. He came out on that resurrection morning not wearing 'clothes', yet He was not seen naked because he had been clothed with incorruption.

His resurrected body is now in His being, and His spirit is no longer inside His body. That was the divine order of life.

What am I saying? When Paul speaks of his house or Tabernacle, he speaks of a garment, the new body. That new body is in heaven, and heaven is your spirit. That body is going to shoot forth from your being. The spirit will overwhelm the body again; what was dead will be dematerialised, and the new body will emerge.

This is how immortality will swallow up mortality. Immortality is who you are in your real essence. Your body is dead because of sin, but your spirit is LIFE because of righteousness. However, because the Spirit that raised Jesus dwells in you, that same Spirit gives life to your mortal body.

> *"And if Christ be in you, the BODY is DEAD because of SIN; but the Spirit is LIFE because of RIGHTEOUSNESS"* (Romans 8:10).

Your heavenly body is not going to come from anywhere outside of you. It is your spirit man coming to overshadow your body. That is what will bring about the swallowing up of mortality by immortality (life-you).

> *"But if the Spirit of him that raised up Jesus from the dead dwell in you, he that raised up Christ from the dead shall also quicken your mortal bodies by his Spirit that dwelleth in you"* (Roms 8:9.

The Spirit that dwells in you is the Spirit of resurrection. That Spirit is ONE with you.

- **That Spirit is you dwelling in your body.**
- **The Holy Spirit is in you by the Spirit that you are.**
- **You are ONE Spirit with the Lord.**

When Jesus rose from the dead, He went to the grave to pick up His body. But note that He picked up a translated brand-new body. How? The new quickening spirit made contact with the former body, and that body was changed. The elements of the former body were absorbed or dissolved, and the new spirit overshadowed that body, creating a new one. This new body is not made of the elements or dust of the earth. It is born of God. It is made of the substance of immortality!

At the resurrection, Jesus offered His blood before the Father. As High Priest, He needed a garment to officiate. He could not have entered the Immortal Tabernacle as a naked spirit or with a fallen Adamic body. When I say naked, I mean without the new body. Nakedness is not the absence of physical clothing. It is the absence of glory.

That was one curse that came from the fall. To be naked is to be without glory. To be without glory is to be without a living body. To be without glory is to be MORTAL, spiritually dead. That was why Jesus said, *"A body you have prepared for me"* Even in his human state, he had a body that could carry out certain functions. His body was spiritual. He wore clothes to appear like those He came to save.

His body was alive. What I mean is that His body did not have sin. He is the spotless Lamb of God who takes away the sin of the world. His body was not subject to corruption, even though it was not immortal. It was a body suited to bear the sin of the world.

The Bible says that His clothing shone as pure light when He manifested Himself on the Mount of Transfiguration. That was the overshadowing of His spirit upon his body. He was not a dead spirit like those he came to redeem, so His body was not dead because of sin. He had a sinless body to bear the sins of men. He was the last Adam.

In the New Testament, we who are LIFE are enjoined to present our bodies as a living sacrifice. God recognises that life is supposed to enter this present body and reverse the course of death therein. That is what the revelation of Jesus should carry out within us. Turn the death-doomed body into a revitalised body and immortalise it!

Aaron's priesthood was not a true reflection of the immortal priesthood, which God is because priesthood gives life, and the very life a high priest gives is himself. A High Priest who is unable to give life is not a TRUTH HIGH PRIEST, BUT A HIGH PRIEST AFTER THE ORDER OF CARNAL COMMANDMENTS. For a TRUTH HIGH PRIEST is he who is ABOVE DEATH.

Our physical body is called a 'death-doomed body'. It's a body that death has worked upon, and a priest cannot officiate with such a body. That is why Paul says we groan to be clothed. He says, "We want to be CLOTHED WITH OUR PRIESTHOOD GARMENT..."

This was what Paul meant when he said in the scripture.

> *"That I may know him, and the power of his resurrection, and the fellowship of his sufferings, being made conformable unto his death; If by any means I might attain unto the resurrection of the dead" (Philippians 3:10-11).*

The Bliss Of Immortality

The Resurrection Of The Dead Is The Resurrection Of The Body.

Now, the garment of our priesthood is white. White means RIGHTEOUSNESS. OUR SPIRIT IS RIGHTEOUSNESS. OUR PRESENT BODY NEEDS TO BE COVERED IN THE RIGHTEOUS STATE OF THE SPIRIT MAN FOR US TO FUNCTION IN THE FULL CAPACITY OF OUR PRIESTHOOD. Righteousness is who you are in Christ Jesus.

That garment from the spirit man (heaven) will wear the body and turn it into a GLORIFIED BODY. All saints who died and left their bodies behind will return with the Lord to pick up those bodies for the bodies to experience RESURRECTION, WHICH IS IMMORTALIZING THE BODY.

The truth is that the body does not have to fall/drop dead to have this experience. The quickening experience by the SPIRIT WHO RAISED JESUS FROM THE DEAD IS NOT RESERVED FOR THE GRAVE. The Lord is saying YOU CAN SWITCH INTO YOUR GLORIFIED body WITHOUT THE BODY DYING PHYSICALLY.

No TRUE PRIEST officiates without his glorified body. So when Jesus came to pick up His body, He overwhelmed the old body, dissolved it and wore the new body, which is also HIS HIGH

PRIEST GARMENT, for officiating in the TABERNACLE of the IMMORTALITY.

If you observe, He did not take the clothing; He was covered in the tomb. It was because he no longer needed it. HE HAD COME INTO A NEW ORDER, IMMORTAL ORDER: the Melchizedek Priesthood.

Our glorified body is translucent. It can reflect the light nature of the spirit man. It does not need any external covering. It is not made of the dust of the earth; it is made of the substances of light, unapproachable. We are unleavened bread. Hallelujah!

CHAPTER 15

Questions

Question 1:

How is my spirit personality the Holy Spirit?

Does that mean I don't have a spirit, but rather have the Holy Spirit as my spirit? If yes, see this:

> *The Spirit bears witness with our spirit. Romans 8:16.*
>
> *"He that is joined to the Lord is one spirit with Him" (1 Cor 6:17).*
>
> *"And the Lord is that Spirit" (2 Cor 3:17).*

Question 2:
What Spirit?

The Spirit of the Lord, which is the Spirit of Christ.

The believer is not a spirit joined to the Lord like you join a man and a woman in a marital union. That is not the reality of our union with God. That is two different persons agreeing to a covenant. It does not really make them ONE in this sense of God and His sons.

The believer is not a dormant spirit inhabited by another spirit called God! That is division.

The believer is vitally and organically ONE with the Lord. They are ONE inseparable entity.

"Whenever you say the Holy Ghost told me" The truth is that He spoke in you, by you, as you because of union:

- Your immortal being is Him
- Your immortal being knows His mind
- Your immortal being communicates and resonates in oneness with DIVINITY

This knowledge of the Oneness is what is being documented in the soul.

The Spirit of Christ is who the believer is. The believer does not have two spirits living inside him. He is Christ.

The Holy Ghost is the Word. The Word is the Father. The Father is the Holy Ghost. These three bear witness to LIFE; therefore, they are ONE SPIRIT. In the beginning was the Word, and the Word was with God, and the Word was God. This is the mystery of ONE.

Jesus said, *"Father, I pray that they might be ONE IN US..." (John 17:21)*.

THE BELIEVER BECAME ONE IN GOD. The human spirit believes in Jesus and is swallowed up into God. He is no more. A new Spirit is brought forth. This New Spirit is the EXPRESS IMAGE of God. 'Express image' also means 'visible form'. The Spirit of the believer is the visible person of God.

> *"The Spirit itself beareth witness with our spirit, that we are the children of God" (Romans 8:16)*.

So the Holy Spirit, in oneness with you as Him, upholds the witness or testimony of God. You were baptised into the Spirit and became INSEPARABLY JOINED TO HIM.

Their witness is their LIFE, and wherever this life is present, God's witness is present. God's witness is His very self, which the believer is.

What you call the Holy Ghost is God indwelling your body. God is you, and you are Christ.

You are that spirit. This concept cannot be adequately taught or explained in human language. You must see it to know it!

That Spirit called 'Christ' is also the Holy Ghost, and it is also the believer. They are all one Spirit. We are now well aware of the Fatherhood of God.

He who sanctified us has begotten us unto a lively hope. He is our Father and Lord. We know Him as such, and we recognise His Fatherhood. We are also aware of our oneness in His Person and how our Spirit witnesses this oneness. The spirit that we are is the witness. The witness is eternal life.

That spirit called 'God' is the very spirit of our being. That is the Spirit at work in us. He worketh in us both to will and to do of His good pleasure. God is doing exceedingly abundantly, far above all we could ever ask or think, according to the power at work in us.

Question 3:

What Is The Power At Work In Us?

For unto us, Christ is made;

- Wisdom
- Righteousness
- Redemption
- Sanctification

This is the power at work in us.

We do not have the righteousness of God. We are the righteousness of God. We do not have the wisdom of God. We are the wisdom of God. We are not going to be sanctified. We are sanctified forever.

> "Elect according to the foreknowledge of God, through sanctification of the spirit unto obedience and sprinkling of the blood of Jesus Christ" (I Peter 1:2).

If any man is in Christ, all things are new, and all things are of God. I want to emphasise that the believer is NOT a dormant spirit inhabited by the Holy Ghost. He is that very Ghost of God.

Jesus told Philip, *"Have you been with me all this while, and yet you do not know the Father? If you have seen me, you have seen the father."* It's the mystery of ONE. It is also true of the believer. If you see me as I am in Him, you have seen the Father.

Hence, the scripture says that we shall be like Him when we see Him. What does this mean? When we see Him as He is in us, when the revelation of Him as He is in us becomes documented in our body and soul, we shall bring forth the manifestation of Him in His resurrected state.

The witness of the Spirit is in the believer, just as that same witness is in the Father and the Son.

Question 4:

Why does scripture say May the Lord sanctify you wholly, your spirit, soul and body 1 Thess. 5:23?

The issue of "the Lord will sanctify us wholly" points to what has happened in us as brand-new beings taking effect in our souls and bodies. That's what the scripture is saying. It doesn't mean God will sanctify the believer sometime in the future.

The life that you are is the testimony of God, and it communicates the will of the Father into your body and soul. That scripture uses the word "wholly". That wholly is speaking of the wholeness of the New Man finding full expression. What is the wholeness of the new man? It manifests God, my spirit, in my body and soul. Bringing this reality to the body and soul region.

The believer is sanctified forever in Christ. Christ is made unto us sanctification. It's not a future event. It is a perfect reality.

Look At This Scripture

> *He that is born of God does not sin, but he keepeth himself and the wicked one toucheth him not.*

That posture of keeping yourself is what is meant by sanctification. That is bringing your members into your sanctification. That is what the scripture in 2 Corinthians 7:1 is talking about.

Question 5:

If our spirit is the Holy Spirit, why are we asked to cleanse it in the scriptures?

> *"Having therefore these promises, dearly beloved, let us cleanse ourselves from all filthiness of the flesh and spirit, perfecting holiness in the fear of God" (2 Corinthians 7:1).*

You keep your members, which are your body and soul, from being touched by the wicked one, is the "cleansing" or "sanctification" or "keeping" that scripture is referring to.

It is the responsibility of the SPIRIT, which is in union with the Godhead, to mortify the members and keep them from all uncleanness. Uncleanness speaks of the unrenewed mind.

> *"That ye put off concerning the former conversation the old man, which is corrupt according to the deceitful lusts; And be renewed in the spirit of your mind"* (Ephesians 4:22).

The unrenewed mind is spiritual. It is an invisible faculty that functions in the Spirit Realm.

Yielding this faculty as an instrument of righteousness is the cleansing that the scripture talks about. When the soul faculty is given to serve the works of the flesh, it engages in the filthiness of the flesh and the spirit. It refers to impurities affecting both body and soul.

- There are sins we commit with the mind
- There are sins we commit with the body

That scripture says to put off the deeds and conversations of the OLD MAN. Those are the contaminations of the spirit. No, they are not contaminated by your spirit or in your spirit. They are spiritual contaminations of the unrenewed mind.

What does that mean? It means they are points of contact for fallen spirits to influence the soul.

Talking about the filthiness of the spirit, it is never the new creation man. It refers to the spiritual uncleanness that is found in the soul. The soul is a spiritual faculty.

There is a translation that says filthiness of the flesh and spirit.

Question 6:

So, are you saying I no longer have a spirit? Is God now my spirit?

'If any man be in Christ, he is a New Creation. Old things have passed away. Behold all things have become new, and all things are of God.'

Also, "We have received the Spirit which is of God that we might know the things that are freely given to us."

That same scripture shows us that it is impossible to know the things of God except you are the Spirit of God.

The new creation is not one with God. The New Creation is ONE IN GOD. You are the Spirit, which is OF GOD.

The Holy Ghost, God, and Christ Jesus are not separate spirit entities. God is the same Spirit called the Holy Ghost, and the same applies to Christ. Christ is who the believer is.

Question 7:

How are we, Christ?

When I say I am Christ, I am just accepting the position offered to me by birth in the Godhead. That does not mean that Jesus Christ no longer exists. I am saying I exist in Him, and He is in me as ONE SPIRIT.

> "And if ye be Christ's, then are ye Abraham's seed, and heirs according to the promise" Galatians 3:29

This scripture says that we are the "seed" of Abraham, not seeds but seed. The scripture below is called 'Christ Jesus, the Seed of Abraham.' He is the seed of Abraham. We are the seed of Abraham. How is that?

> *"Now to Abraham and his seed were the promises made. He saith not, And to seeds, as of many; but as of one, And to thy seed, which is Christ" (Galatians 3:16).*

The personality called 'Christ' comprises 'Head and Body'. There is Jesus Christ. He is the Head, while the believer is the Body. You cannot use the relationship between husband and wife to explain the indivisible union of Christ and believers.

We cannot use human life to explain our union with divinity or our placement in the Godhead. Believers are not like human beings.

When Jesus said, *"Some will come in my name, saying, 'I am Christ,'"* He referred to people who deny Him as Lord but present themselves as Christ to others, claiming to be the ones who would save and deliver them from their troubles.

They deny the Spirit and Lordship of Christ, and yet present themselves to people as the prophet who is to come after Jesus. They seek to command followership after themselves, not after the Lamb. They point men to themselves. They do not know Christ and do not acknowledge God's finished work. They set themselves as God over other men and command worship from them. This is a lying Spirit. We have seen many such things in our time. I'd rather not mention names.

The Antichrist Spirit will claim to be Christ but will never acknowledge Christ's lordship or the supremacy of the finished work. That is the Spirit that denies that God has come in the flesh! A spirit that demands the worship and followership of men to turn them away from the Lamb.

But we are Christ by our joint heirship with Him, THE CHRIST! We are the Begotten. He is our BEGETTER who has begotten us unto a lively hope and has made us partakers of His Divine Nature! We are in love with this Lamb!

There is only one progenitor of the new creation race, Jesus Christ. All were in Him when He was born as the new man. If you are in Him, He is the Spirit that you are!

Brethren, that scripture is never a reference to those whose hearts are captured by Jesus, who love Him, who acknowledge their oneness in Him, who acknowledge His Lordship, who are called by His name. My being Christ is in union with Him, not detachment from Him! My power and authority lie in my union with Him and in Him! Therefore, I am CHRIST!

Blessings!

Question 8:
Does it mean the believer can never go to hell?

Let me bring some clarity here.

The Bliss Of Immortality

> *"If any man sees his brother sin a sin which is not unto death, he shall ask, and he shall give him life for them that sin not unto death. There is a sin unto death: I do not say that he shall pray for it." All unrighteousness is sin, and there is a sin not unto death. We know that whosoever is born of God sinneth not, but he that is begotten of God keepeth himself, and that wicked one toucheth him not. And we know that we are of God and the whole world lieth in wickedness. And we know that the Son of God is come, and hath given us an understanding, that we may know him that is true, and we are in him that is true, even in his Son Jesus Christ. This is the true God and eternal life. Little children, keep yourselves from idols. Amen. (1 John 5:16-21).*

A saint cannot commit the sin that is unto death. That is the kind of sin Adam committed. That is the sin that relocates a man or a spirit entity from light into darkness. You can't commit such a sin without the stature of a progenitor. Adam was the seed bearer for the generation of the First Man, and all who were in him were to partake of his fruit.

A progenitor, as I am referring to here, is the father of a race. Adam was such because he was the father of the human race. The last Adam was also a progenitor, although he did not procreate in his state of living soul. He brought forth his kind in His state as the Life-Giving Spirit. I am His kind. Satan could tempt Him the way he tempted Adam because Jesus Christ was a progenitor, a seed bearer.

The Sin Of A Progenitor

The sin of a progenitor is a sin that plunges an entire race within a progenitor into death. It is a corporate sin. One man sinned, and his entire seed or generation was corrupted. This will help us to understand the scripture below.

> "For as in Adam all died, even so in Christ shall all be made alive" (1 Corinthians 15:22).

Adam's sin is the only sin that brought all men into condemnation, which is spiritual death. Every other sin was not the reason why Jesus came to earth. Jesus came to earth primarily because, in Adam, all died. That is what the scripture above states. By the sin of one man, all came into condemnation. That is the sin unto death. Take a look at the scripture below.

> "For as by one man's disobedience many were made sinners, so by the obedience of one shall many be made righteous" (Romans 5:19).

After the fall of Adam, some men sought God and walked with him. Despite that, no matter how righteous their acts, they could not attain eternal salvation. Why?

All have sinned, not because of acts but because of acquired nature. All were dead in Adam.

> "Therefore, as by the offence of one judgment came upon all men to condemnation; even so by the righteousness of one the free gift came upon all men unto justification of life" (Romans 5:18).

The Bliss Of Immortality

No man before Christ crossed from death to life. It was not their sin that put them in that state. It was the sin of their father, Adam.

> *"For if through the offence of one many be dead, much more the grace of God, and the gift by grace, which is by one man, Jesus Christ, hath abounded unto many" (Romans 5:15).*

Likewise, it is not the righteousness of a man that offers him eternal redemption. It is faith in the finished work. When a person is in Christ, they have become righteous. He has crossed from death to life because of the ONE MAN by whom all have been justified and made alive. A believer cannot commit the sin that will bring him out of Christ back into condemnation. The believer did not just receive salvation; we BECAME salvation. Salvation is a Being; God is salvation. When God gives you a blessing, you become that blessing in essence. God does not just attach something to you so that you can easily lose it. He makes you the very thing. We do not have righteousness; we are righteousness. We do not have wisdom. We are wisdom. Our being is a blessing that cannot be thrown away as if it is corrupt!

> *"Therefore, as by the offence of one judgment came upon all men to condemnation; even so by the righteousness of one the free gift came upon all men unto justification of life" (Romans 5:18).*

The descendants of Adam and Christ are not, by nature, progenitors. No descendant of Adam can achieve the righteousness God requires to transition from death to life. Similarly, no descendant of Christ can sin, capable of transitioning from life to death.

To commit such a sin, you must be the carrier of the seed of an entire race. You must be a man of such stature, bearing the seed of a whole generation. Though Abraham was called the Father of many nations that notwithstanding, he was not the progenitor of the human race. Adam was.

Check the first and the last Adam. They were, by nature, progenitors. They were both fathers of a race.

The sin of a progenitor cannot be committed in ignorance. It is done in the light of knowledge. It is the sin of a kind of "High Priest", not just one who officiates in a temple, but one who bears an entire race in his loins. He bears the scroll of generations in his loins from the hand of Him who sits on the throne. He stands before God as the Portal of Immortality. Such a High Priest is He who can commit the sin that is unto death to plunge himself and his entire seed into death.

When such a sin is committed, it requires more than forgiveness to merit freedom from its effects, because forgiveness alone cannot handle it. It is a matter of judgment. It is a matter of remission. Blood must be shed. God's judgment must come upon the entire race that sinned because it is not just an act but a mutation of nature. It is a switch from one dimension to another. It is a sin that must be judged because it has to do with a change of nature, not just an expression of nature.

For example, Adam sinned as a progenitor in the light of knowledge. His race did not commit that manner of sin; they expressed the sin nature their Father Adam passed on to them.

The significant effect of the sin of a progenitor is the impartation of the nature of spiritual DEATH.

You can now understand why forgiveness of sin cannot erase the effect of the sin of a progenitor. The effect requires the life of another progenitor, one with a profile of PURITY AND INNOCENCE from the condemnation that all came into.

Jesus came as a higher Progenitor for the redemption of Adam and his offspring from death unto life eternal. 1 Cor 15. He came to make a switch from death into life, not for himself but for all who died in Adam. He became the worthy Lamb because he had no condemnation.

He was made in the likeness of sinful flesh, so He became us. He identified with us. He entered a union with humanity that made Him one with humanity in the state of death. He was tempted, too, like the first Adam. He was tempted at every point, but he was found without sin. So the sin He bore was not His sin (He had none) but the sin of a race that died in Adam. The nature of death was imputed to Him. Therefore, all who died in Adam were located in him.

Again, the sin of a Progenitor cannot be forgiven. It must be judged and TAKEN AWAY. The forgiveness of the sin is in its being TAKEN AWAY because until blood is shed, there is no remission or removal of this kind of sin. Even when the blood of bulls and goats was shed, they could not purge the conscience of sin consciousness. The people were still in bondage to the law of sin and death. It would require a mediator to take away the nature of sin in man.

Look At The Scriptures Below

> "For then must he often have suffered since the foundation of the world: but now once in the end of the world hath he appeared to put away sin by the sacrifice of himself. So Christ was once offered to bear the sins of many; and unto them that look for him shall he appear the second time without sin unto salvation" (Hebrews 9:26-28).

> "Nevertheless death reigned from Adam to Moses, even over them that had not sinned AFTER THE SIMILITUDE OF ADAM'S TRANSGRESSION, who is the figure of him that was to come" (Romans 5:14, KJV).

There is the SIMILITUDE OF ADAM'S TRANSGRESSION. When Adam sinned, it was a transmutation. This shift was not personal; it affected the entire human race. But when Cain sinned, he expressed a nature inherited from the sin of Adam.

> "Wherefore, as by one man sin entered into the world, and death by sin; and so death passed upon all men, for that all have sinned" (Romans 5:12).

The Bliss Of Immortality

God did not forgive Adam's sin. It is not a sin to be forgiven (Pls understand me). It is a sin to be blotted out. Someone must receive the punishment for such sin on behalf of Adam and his race before it can be taken away. It must be taken away. Jesus is the Lamb of God that TAKETH AWAY the sin of the world. He did not just forgive the sin of the world;

THE SIN OF THE WORLD IS THE SIN OF ADAM. JESUS TOOK IT AWAY.

Adam suffered the consequence of sin, but he could not bear it and take it away because he was under condemnation. It would take a kind of man who is not under condemnation to take away the sin of the world, the Spotless Lamb.

> "Who his own self bare our sins in his own body on the tree, that we, being dead to sins, should live unto righteousness: by whose stripes ye were healed" (1 Peter 2:24).

The healing here is, first and foremost, healing from the nature of sin, which is the reason for soul and body-related diseases. No believer can commit this kind of sin, brethren. No saint can cross back from Christ into condemnation all by himself. Why? It was not by his righteousness that he came into Christ. He only believed. AND BY BELIEVING, THE OLD MAN WAS EXTERMINATED. A NEW BEING IN A NEW STATE IS BORN!

This is what it means to sin: to pass from life to death. To sin is to enter condemnation. That is why there is, therefore, NOW NO CONDEMNATION. FOR THOSE WHO ARE IN CHRIST JESUS WHO WALK NOT AFTER THE FLESH BUT AFTER THE SPIRIT.

THE BELIEVER IS NOT IN THE FLESH. HE IS IN THE SPIRIT. TO BE IN THE FLESH IS TO BE IN CONDEMNATION, which is spiritual death.

However, because we have not yet reached full knowledge and maturity, we live below our potential as Christ. We err. We slip, and we err in our thinking. Why? The mind needs to be swallowed up by the revelation of OUR IMMORTAL IDENTITY.

The saint must put on the MIND OF CHRIST for acts of sin to stop, and we can grow up to the point of blameless conduct. A perfect response to truth is possible. The limitations, constraints, and fear of the invisible dimensions, all effects of the fall (sin), can all be stripped off as we behold the revelation of our reality as Christ.

The new creation man CANNOT BE TEMPTED. CANNOT SIN. CANNOT FALL. This is our reality, and this reality is manifest as we put on the MIND OF GOD.

Some other conditions do not appear to be sin, but are effects of sin: spiritual dullness, inability to relate to invisible realities, and religious thinking. Most people who do not fornicate, steal or feel more righteous than those who do, yet many like that are so dull spiritually and full of religious inclinations.

When a saint is not exposed to light, such would live as one who has not been delivered from the power of sin and the limitations that came by the fall. But when we set the understanding of truth before the saints, they live out the reality they behold. We should teach and preach nothing but the righteousness of God to believers.

So when we err, we receive help and press on in the light. As we grow in understanding that the Holy Ghost gives (understanding judges us and aligns us with the reality of our identity), we naturally move beyond errors and begin to yield fruits. We begin to walk worthy of the Lord UNTO ALL PLEASING.

We are perfect because of what God accomplished in Christ, but we do not suddenly produce perfection in our conduct and actions. Maturity and perfection in conduct come as we continually behold the light of the glory of God, responding to every dealing that the light is designed to work into us. The Lord knows this, and He is patient with us all.

Those who continue to willfully sin after they have been born of God are ignorant of their immortal identity. Teach them! Those who continue to sin after the light of truth has shone upon them have not yet understood the truth. They are filled with undigested head knowledge. They are not truly fellowshipping with that truth they have seen because truth sets free. They know, but they have not truly known. Intercede for them.

The error of our ways and thoughts and our inappropriate responses to truth are "the sin that is not unto death."

As believers, we are born again not of a corruptible seed, but of an INCORRUPTIBLE SEED, the IMMORTAL WORD OF GOD which liveth and abideth FOREVER, which does not die, which CANNOT BE REVERSED FROM LIFE BACK INTO DEATH. AMEN

Glory to God!

Question 9:

But why does Romans 2:7 say 'to those seeking immortality?

We do not seek immortality. Rom 2:7 is not a reference to begotten sons. The wrong presentation of Romans 2:7 has put many believers on an endless journey of looking for immortality, a state in which they are already being born of the immortal word of God. James 1:18. New Testament saints do not seek immortality. We are immortality and life now.

We are the immortal, visible image of the immortal, invisible God. As Christ is, so are we in this world. Scripture must be accurately divided in this season.

> "To them who by patient continuance in well doing seek for glory and honour and immortality, eternal life" (Rom. 2:7).

If you carefully look at the scripture above, you will notice that it does not refer to believers. There is no way it could have been referring to believers, because believers already possess eternal life. Hebrews 3:1 calls believers partakers of the heavenly calling. The heavenly calling is immortality promised to Abraham in Christ.

Question 10:

Do You Seek What You Already Have? No!

As you examine that scripture closely, you will also notice that it states immortality is equivalent to eternal life. The words immortality and eternal life mean the same thing—any attempt to separate the two words breeds error.

If that scripture had said, "immortality and eternal life," it would have meant that immortality and eternal life refer to two different things. But it says, "Immortality, eternal life". English students will explain it better.

Let's Look At The Scripture Again

> "To them who by patient continuance in well doing seek for glory and honour and immortality, eternal life" (Rom. 2:7).

The scripture says, "to them." Who are "them" here? It is a question we should all first ask ourselves. Does the word "them" refer to Old Testament saints or New Testament saints?

The word "seek" in that scripture is what has caused confusion for many. The word "seek for" should have been translated as "sought for" Follow me carefully, please.

Now, if you substitute the word "seek for" with the word "sought for", you will immediately know who the word "them" in the above scripture refers to.

Please Read That Scripture Like This.

> "To them who by patient continuance in well doing sought" for glory and honour and immortality, eternal life" (Rom. 2:7).

Do not forget that the next verse speaks of some who did not seek this immortality under the old covenant. Check it out below.

> "But unto them that are contentious, and do not obey the truth, but obey unrighteousness, indignation and wrath, tribulation and anguish, upon every soul of man that doeth evil, of the Jew first, and also of the gentile" (Romans 2:8-9).

Paul was addressing an issue that has to do with both Jews and Gentiles, not the Church.

When you say "sought for" glory, honour, immortality, and eternal life, it gives you the proper perspective. I will provide a scripture to help you understand what I am saying. Check the scripture below.

> "And these all, having obtained a good report through faith, received not the promise: god having provided some better thing for us, that they without us should not be made perfect" (Hebrews 11:39-40).

The Bliss Of Immortality

This scripture refers to the Old Testament, which relates to men and women. It states that they received a good report but did not fulfil the promise.

Question 11:

What, Then, Is The Promise?

The promise is God's righteousness and eternal life. Righteousness, which is eternal life, is immortality. The word 'immortality' captures the invisible essence of the uncreated God. This uncreated life or state of being of God in the immortal reality is what God promised Abraham. That was what some Old Testament saints (not all of them) sought.

They are the "them" in Romans 2:7 who "sought for" immortality, which is eternal life through their good deeds. The New Testament believers are partakers of what some Old Testament saints sought through their well-doing.

Their well-doing could only earn them good reports. Their well-being could not impact their immortality, which is eternal life. The scripture below states that in Christ, all who died in Adam will be made alive and partake of the divine, immortal nature of God.

Don't forget that the scripture says that Papa Abraham looked for a city whose builder and maker is God.

> *"By faith he sojourned in the land of promise, as in a strange country, dwelling in tabernacles with Isaac and Jacob, the heirs with him of the same promise: for he looked for a city*

which hath foundations, whose builder and maker is God" (Hebrews 11:9-10).

According to the scripture above, the city is not a nation or continent. The city Abraham sought is righteousness, which is the immortal nature of God.

This nature was offered to all men through the seed of Abraham, Christ.

Check The Scripture Below, Please

"Christ hath redeemed us from the curse of the law, being made a curse for us: for it is written, cursed is everyone that hangeth on a tree that the blessing of Abraham might come on the Gentiles through Jesus Christ; that we might receive the promise of the spirit through faith" (Galatians 3:13-14).

What is the blessing, not blessings of Abraham, which the above scripture says was to come on the Gentiles?

Check The Scripture Below, Please

"Now to Abraham and his seed were the promises made. He saith not, and to seeds, as of many; but as of one, and to thy seed, which is Christ" (Galatians 3:16).

This scripture states that the promise made to Abraham is about his seed, and his seed is Christ. Christ is the immortality revealed in the gospel of God, after death was abolished, as stated in 2 Timothy 1:9-11 in the New International Version (NIV).

The Bliss Of Immortality

"He has saved us and called us to a holy life—not because of anything we have done but because of his own purpose and grace. This grace was given us in Christ Jesus before the beginning of time, but it has now been revealed through the appearing of our Saviour, Christ Jesus, who has destroyed death and has brought life and immortality to light through the gospel. And of this gospel I was appointed a herald and an apostle and a teacher."

Look At This Scripture Below, Please.

Behold the conclusion of the whole matter.

> *"For ye are all the children of God by faith in Christ Jesus. For as many of you as have been baptised into Christ have put on Christ. And if ye be Christ's, then are ye Abraham's seed and heirs according to the promise"* (Galatians 3:26-27,29).

Please read the above well. It states that we, the New Testament saints, are the children or sons of God by faith in Jesus Christ. What do you think that is?

Read on. It further states that as many as are baptised into Christ have put on Christ. Did you see that?

What does it mean to put on Christ? To put on Christ is to put on immortality because Christ is the immortality revealed in the flesh.

If you say you have put on Christ through the new birth experience, but you do not have immortality yet, it shows you are unaware of the Christ you have put on.

Hebrews 1:3 states that Christ is the brightness of the glory of the immortal God and the exact representation of His invisible nature; that is, He possesses immortality, brethren.

Please look at this scripture below.

> *Galatians 3:29 says that "And if ye (you) be Christ's, then are ye(you) Abraham's seed (Christ) and heirs (immortality) according to the promise (to Abraham)."*

We are immortality now. We are life no. We are the visible image of God revealed to creation now. Define your identity from the perspective of your life now, and then tell us if you are an immortal or a mortal human being.

I am alive and immortal now!

An end to all controversy.

The Bliss Of Immortality

Reflection Point

Personal Notes: _____

Guided Action Plan

www.ingramcontent.com/pod-product-compliance
Lightning Source LLC
Chambersburg PA
CBHW031834230426
43669CB00009B/1348